Finding God in the Ordinary

# Finding God in the Ordinary

Pierce Taylor Hibbs

WIPF & STOCK · Eugene, Oregon

FINDING GOD IN THE ORDINARY

Wipf & Stock
An Imprint of Wipf and Stock Publishers
199 W. 8th Ave., Suite 3
Eugene, OR 97401

www.wipfandstock.com

PAPERBACK ISBN: 978-1-5326-5768-9
HARDCOVER ISBN: 978-1-5326-5769-6
EBOOK ISBN: 978-1-5326-5770-2

Manufactured in the U.S.A.

*For my wife, who walks with me through the ordinary*

## Other Books by the Author

*The Trinity, Language, and Human Behavior:
A Reformed Exposition of the Language
Theory of Kenneth L. Pike*

*In Divine Company: Growing Closer to the
God Who Speaks*

*Theological English: An Advanced ESL Text
for Students of Theology*

*The Speaking Trinity & His Worded World:
Why Language Is at the Center of Everything*

Visit piercetaylorhibbs.com to read more
from this author and to receive updates
about new publications.

# Contents

# Introduction

OVER THE YEARS, I have been blessed to receive a biblically sound theological education.[1] I have learned much about God and his world in light of the truth of Scripture. Yet, I have also noticed that even those of us who have special training in theology are susceptible to a sort of numbness or a lack of awe and worship in our daily lives. In fact, perhaps this is an even greater threat for those who study theology than it is for those who work in other professions. And this is no small thing: how can we possibly lose a sense of awe and wonder when we claim to have a personal relationship with the Father, Son, and Holy Spirit?

I believe that, like it or not, all of us are negatively affected by the sinful world in which we live. We strive not to be, and we prayerfully ask God's help in enabling us to be *in* the world but not *of* the world. Still, our hearts and minds can easily become infected by unbiblical thinking when we are not being vigilant, that is, when we are not earnestly engaging with God and his word every day.

Now, what exactly does this sort of negative worldly effect look like? I believe that it takes the form of "neutrality" or "impersonal objectivity." Let me explain what I mean.

---

1. I completed an MAR degree at Westminster Theological Seminary in 2010, and finished my ThM degree at the same institution in 2016. I cannot say enough to commend this school for its biblical integrity and its commitment to Reformed theology.

For people who do not believe that a tripersonal God has spoken the world into being and maintains all things by the word of his power (Gen 1:1; Heb 1:3; John 1:1; Col 1:17), the world can seem like a conglomeration of elements: a tree here, a building there—a daisy, a duck, a daydream. All of these things are basically phenomena detached from any meaningful plan of a God who knows you and me on an intimate level. Apart from the life-giving work of the Holy Spirit, who unites us to Christ by faith and reconciles us to our heavenly Father, the world looks as if it is *just there*. It looks cold and impersonal and void of any unified purpose.

This is perhaps one of the greatest falsehoods that the devil uses to keep people spiritually crippled. And this falsehood has been given fodder by the empirical and rationalistic tendencies in modern life and thought.[2] "The world," says Satan, "is *just there*. It's just a cold and neutral atmosphere in which you eek out your miserable, doubt-laden life. There is no God here." As Christians, we know this is a bold-faced lie. God himself has told us, in his word, that he is both transcendent and immanent.[3] He is both Lord over all things and yet intimately close to all of us. In fact, the tripersonal God is even *in* those who believe in the name of Christ (John 14:23; Rom. 8:9). He is *that* close.

According to Scripture, the world is not cold and impersonal. In fact, it has been marked by its maker, a warm and personal God. In Romans 1, Paul speaks of the ungodly and unrighteous and says that "what can be known about God is plain to them, because God has shown it to them. For his invisible attributes, namely, his eternal power and divine nature, have been clearly perceived, ever since the creation of the world, *in the things that have been made*" (Rom. 1:19–20; emphasis added). The world in which we live reveals God. Notice that Paul is simple here. His expression covers all of creation: "the things that have been made," that is, *everything*.

2. For a helpful Christian approach to the way in which empiricism and rationalism are examples of rebellion against the God who is fully present with us, see Frame, *A History of Western Philosophy and Theology*.

3. On God's transcendence and immanence, see Frame, *The Doctrine of the Knowledge of God*, 13–18; *The Doctrine of God*, 103–15.

It is not the case that some of the world reveals God, or even that most of it does; *all* of creation is marked by the triune God who spoke it into being and maintains it by the word of his power.

This means, among other things, that the world is *revelational* of God. It reveals him, and in that sense "speaks" of him. This does not mean that the world is animated or that pantheism is biblically warranted. It simply means that the world is not mute and cold. It testifies to the Lord who made it and sustains it. Psalm 19:1–4 is unabashed about this.

> The heavens declare the glory of God,
>
> and the sky above proclaims his handiwork.
>
> ² Day to day pours out speech,
>
> and night to night reveals knowledge.
>
> ³ There is no speech, nor are there words,
>
> whose voice is not heard.
>
> ⁴ Their voice goes out through all the earth,
>
> and their words to the end of the world.

There is a profound sense in which all of the world "speaks" of God, in that it reveals something about him. John Calvin is one my major influences on this point, though he was merely voicing the truth of Scripture:

> Whichever way we turn our eyes, there is no part of the world, however small, in which at least some spark of God's glory does not shine. In particular, we cannot gaze upon this beautiful masterpiece of the world, in all its length and breadth, without being completely dazzled, as it were, by an endless flood of light. Accordingly, in Hebrews, the apostle aptly calls the world the mirror of things invisible, because the structure of the world serves as a mirror in which we behold God, who otherwise cannot be seen (Heb 11:3).⁴

An endless flood of light—that is our world. We are literally surrounded by an environment steeped in God's presence, a world

4. Calvin, *Institutes of the Christian Religion*, 10.

that cannot help but reveal something of the God who spoke it into being. Sin is the reason why we are blinded to this profound truth.

That is why we must constantly rid ourselves of the falsehood that the world is somehow neutral and cold: a conglomeration of elements, unpossessed by God and void of divinely-ordained meaning. Our sinful world says, "The earth is man's; we govern ourselves." But God says, "The earth is the Lord's and the fullness thereof, the world and those who dwell therein" (Ps 24:1). We are living on and within purchased property—an entire cosmos that is possessed and governed by the triune God. And the Father, Son, and Holy Spirit have so created this cosmos that it reveals God's control, authority, and presence around every corner.[5]

This book is my attempt to describe "commonplace" elements or events of my own life and reflect on how they reveal the God I worship and serve. My hope is that this book encourages you to look for God in the world around you—in the ordinary. He is here. And because he is here, the world is not truly ordinary. It is always *extra*ordinary because all around us we find marks of the Trinity: the God who governs, guides, and protects his people in a world that everywhere reveals his presence with us. Let us together train our minds and hearts to combat the sinful assumptions of the world and find the God of grace in the strangest places. This will take daily work on our part, driven and empowered by the Holy Spirit. But we have already been promised by Christ himself that *this* Spirit, living in us, will guide us into all truth (John 16:13).

---

5. The triad of God's control, authority, and presence is one of the many contributions that John Frame has made to Reformed theology. It can be seen throughout his works, but a concise introduction can be found in his *Systematic Theology*, 21–31.

# 1

## The Solar System in My Coffee Cup

ROUTINE HAS A WAY of anesthetizing us to daily detail. We often need something to snap the smelling salts and bring us back to marvel at the world in which we live. One of the ways I bring myself to contemplate the particularities around me is by listening to instrumental piano music. Some people far more educated and experienced in music than I am might call it "new age" or something like that. But all I know is that it makes me think, and that's what I want early in the day.

As the sun was rising one early September morning, the piano notes began to fill the air. I sat at my desk with a cup of black coffee and was just about to start checking email when I glanced at the surface of the coffee in my mug. There were swirls of tiny particles from the coffee grounds churning in circles that intermingled, broke from each other, then interlocked again. I was mesmerized. As the piano music drifted through the room, life seemed to slow to a halt. More and more, the swirling particles looked like galaxies, slow-dancing around some gravitational point, bending and turning, colliding and reshaping.

The blackness of the coffee, contrasting with my white mug, served as a silent and still backdrop for smaller movements, which I had thought were *ordinary*, even irrelevant. But these were not ordinary. Nothing is ordinary or irrelevant in a world that has been birthed into being by the speech of the Trinity, a world which holds together because of that selfsame speech (John 1:1; Heb 1:3).

As I reflected on the swirls in my coffee cup, I thought not about where the coffee had come from or how it tasted. I thought about our solar system. We get so caught up in ourselves that we forget our own smallness. Self-centeredness, you know, is a magnifying behavior. As we think more and more about ourselves, we appear to be more focal, as the rest of the world fades into a fuzzy background. But that is just an appearance. The truth of the matter is that we are tiny—little conscious creatures ambling about in God's greatness. It is in *him* that "we live and move and have our being" (Acts 17:28). But this "him" is vast. We carry on in a cosmos too immense to imagine. As I am drinking my tiny cup of coffee, sitting in my tiny chair, in my tiny office, in a tiny building, there are stars burning, planets rotating on axis, comets soaring through blackness, moons encircling planets. Here I sit with my coffee cup, my microcosm of the cosmos.

I say that I am small, but that does not cover the half of my wonder. What really sets my head spinning is the fact that in this vastness, in this universe too extensive to traverse, too deep to fathom, there is a God who knows my *name* . . . *my* name: Pierce Taylor Hibbs. No matter how old I get, I will always be asking a very simple question: Why? Why does God, who spoke the world into motion and governs every quark and cotton blossom with his speech, why does he know my name? Why does he *want* to know my name? I do not understand. I know all of the theological answers to that question, conceptually. We are made in God's image, bound in covenant with him, made to worship him in the fullness of our personality—but put all of that on hold for just a moment. Think with me about king David's ancient psalm.

> When I look at your heavens, the work of your fingers,
>
> the moon and the stars, which you have set in place,
>
> what is man that you are mindful of him,
>
> and the son of man that you care for him? (Ps 8:3–4)

David likely knew the book of Genesis much better than many of us today. He knew that we are precious to God because we have been made in God's image (Gen 1:26–27), but that did not stop him from marveling. How could it be that the God of heaven and earth, who as I write is helping a hornet tread across a telephone wire outside my window, the Lord of time and space, would want to know *me*? Why would God be *mindful* of me?

The answer to that question is very simple—so simple, in fact, that we neglect it even when we try to think about God. It is an answer both profoundly simple and infinitely mysterious: love. You see, love is not just what God does or how he acts; *love is who God is* (1 John 4:8). God *is* love. This is perhaps a bit easier to approach when we remember that God is the Trinity: the Father, Son, and Holy Spirit.

Dumitru Stăniloae, a Romanian theologian in the Orthodox tradition, wrote a book entitled *The Holy Trinity: In the Beginning There Was Love*.[1] In the beginning, before time and space were spoken into being, before the stars were burning, before the earth was turning, there was *love*. "God is love," he writes, "and therefore life and light in themselves, because he is the supreme unity of three individual persons in communion with one another."[2]

Abraham Kuyper, in the Dutch Reformed tradition, also wrote movingly of the Trinity as the hearth of love.

> God's children have derived from the Word deeper and richer conceptions of divine Love, for they confess a Triune God, Father, Son, and Holy Ghost, one God in three Persons: the Father, who generates; the Son, who is generated; and the Holy Spirit, who proceeds from both Father and Son. And the Love-life whereby these Three mutually love each other is the Eternal Being Himself. This alone is the true and real life of Love. The entire Scripture teaches that nothing is more precious and glorious than the Love of the Father for the Son, and of the Son for the Father, and of the Holy Spirit for both.
>
> This Love is nameless: human tongue has no words to express it; no creature may *inquisitively* look into its eternal depths. It is the great and impenetrable mystery.

1. Stăniloae, *The Holy Trinity: In the Beginning There Was Love*.
2. Stăniloae, 14. I would say "self-conscious" rather than "individual," since the latter could imply that there are three independent beings in God.

We listen to its music and adore it, but when its glory has passed through the soul, the lips are still unable adequately to describe any of its features. God may loose the tongue so that it can shout and sing to the praise of eternal love, but the intellect remains powerless.

Love is not God, but God is love; and He is sufficient to Himself to love absolutely and forever. He has no need of the creature, and the exercise of His Love did not begin with the creature whom He could love, but it flows and springs eternally in the Love-life of the Triune God. God is Love; its perfection, divine beauty, real dimensions, and holiness are not found in men, not even in the best of God's children, but scintillate only around the Throne of God.[3]

God *is* love. And it was this loving, trinitarian God who spoke us into motion and gave us each *a name*.

We are so used to the practice of earthly parents naming their children that we forget this practice has divine roots. God himself, as the Father of Adam, gave the first human his name (Gen 2:20), a named derived from the substance that God had used to form him: dust (Gen 2:7; cf. 3:19; 5:2). God's naming of Adam set the precedent (the image-bearing ability) for Adam to name his wife and children (Gen 3:20, 4:25–26).[4] The name of a person, especially in the biblical tradition, was more than a sound, a sequence of letters. A name was an *identity*, a revelation of sorts. A name, in Herman Bavinck's words, "is a sign of the person bearing it, a designation referring to some characteristic in which a person reveals himself or herself and becomes knowable. There is a connection between a name and its bearer, and that connection, so far from being arbitrary, is rooted in that bearer."[5] Names express something of their bearers.

What's more, name-giving is an exercise in authority. God had named the parts of creation and thereby exercised his authority

---

3. Abraham Kuyper, *The Work of the Holy Spirit*, trans. Henry De Vries (Chattanooga, TN: AMG Publishers, 1995), 542–43.

4. See also Poythress, *In the Beginning Was the Word*, 29–30.

5. Bavinck, *God and Creation*, 97.

and sovereign control. As a derivative example of authority, Adam, as God's image-bearer, was meant to name the creatures God had created. Adam's naming was meant to submit to the Lordship of his maker; it was a "naming that drew the world toward the destiny planned by God from the beginning."[6]

Now, take these twin truths—that names express something of their bearers and that naming is an exercise in authority—and think of your own name. Your name has a revelatory character: by it, you are marked and become *known* to others. But you did not (likely) name yourself. Your parents named you, exercising their God-given parental authority. But that authority, like Adam's name-giving authority, was granted by and is subservient to God's own authority. Ultimately, God is the one who controlled what your name would be. God, in a sense, has named you. He has given you a name, through creating and controlling the circumstances and persons that lead to your birth. Why would God do this?

We go again to the profoundly simple and infinitely mysterious answer: love. In naming Adam (and the rest of us), God exercises his Lordship over us. He claims us as his own, and he does so in *love*. Our names reflect not merely our own identity among human persons but our great meaning and worth among the divine persons of the Godhead. The Father, Son, and Holy Ghost are responsible for your name and mine. And because God *is* love, that responsibility has emerged *from* love. You and I have a name because God is love.

The tripersonal God who is love knows us each by name. Indeed, he has given us our names! And this means that the divine Love-life of the Trinity has spilled over the edges of eternity's cup and covered us. We are saturated with the holy, creative, and redeeming love of God. We may not always feel saturated. In fact, oftentimes we feel dried to the bone, directionless, lifeless even. But the truth of what God has done and is doing in us and through us is not judged by our feelings. It is judged by his word.

Let us return to David's psalm. His burning question was, "What is man that you are mindful of him, and the son of man

6. Poythress, *In the Beginning Was the Word*, 37.

that you care for him?" David, my brother, though it may not seem like much of an answer, God is mindful of us because of his great and mysterious love, a Spirit-forged love in Christ from which we cannot be sundered. With a heart of faith, I say with Paul, "I am sure that neither death nor life, nor angels nor rulers, nor things present nor things to come, nor powers, nor height nor depth, nor anything else in all creation, will be able to separate us from the love of God in Christ Jesus our Lord" (Rom 8:38–39).

This is the great truth that outshines all others. As I stare at the swirling coffee grounds in my mug and think of the vastness of our world, I know that I am very small and yet greatly loved. Perhaps most of the Christian life is about our coming to accept this basic fact. In the greatness of God, the smallest of things is given tremendous weight.

## 2

## Isaac's Giggle

AT THE TIME OF my writing this, my son Isaac is four years old. I say about him what all parents likely say about their own children: Isaac is *special*. More specifically, he is a highly sensitive, deep-feeling little boy. This leads both to blessings and difficulties for him. On one evening, I found great joy in one of the blessings. But I was surprised by it, for it emerged from a seed of sorrow.

Memory is a marvelous and miraculous thing. St. Augustine wrote that memory is comprised of fields and great mansions.[1] Memory is our existential wealth, an estate of sorts, in which we have invested our most prized asset: time. Yet while memory is the estate of our experience, it also brings us grief and regret. Memories can make us melancholy, especially when we view bits of life as irretrievable coins that have fallen through our clumsy fingers. We cannot get the life experience back, only the impression that lives on in our minds. Time is *lost*, and so some things, we assume, are lost and gone forever.

That passing thought can bring us to tears when we experience something striking or beautiful. On one night, we were watching a movie as a family, an old children's movie: *The Land Before Time*. It's a tale about a dinosaur who overcomes adversity and loss to discover "the Great Valley," a land teaming with life, lush with green food and clean, flowing water. At one point in the movie, Isaac (who was mesmerized by the story) watched two of

1. Saint Augustine, *Confessions* 10.12.

7

the characters joking with one another. An innocent giggle tumbled through his smile. My wife and I both looked at each other and grinned at the pure joy we had just heard from the other side of the couch. "I'm going to miss that little laugh one day," I thought. I said something similar to my wife, which made her eyes well up with tears. We hate the idea that something so pure and beautiful, something good, will pass away and never come back. That is the very same notion that is tied up with our hatred of death.

But as we settled back into the movie, I realized I had not considered God as I listened to Isaac giggle. God was listening too. He is ever present. What if I thought about Isaac's laugh living on not only in my memory and in my wife's memory, but in *God's* memory?

I said that memory is a marvelous and miraculous thing, but it is also a divine thing. All throughout Scripture, we read of God's *remembering*. Even the Pentateuch provides scads of references to God's memory. God remembered Noah and the covenant he had made with him (Gen 8:1; 9:15–16). He remembered Abraham (Gen 19:29) and Rachel (Gen 30:22). He remembered his covenant with the patriarchs—Abraham, Isaac, and Jacob—when he heard the Israelites groaning under Egyptian oppression (Exod 2:24; 6:5). He promised to remember that same covenant when his people humbled themselves and repented of their sins (Lev 26:42). God has a memory.

Now, in light of the fact that God is our *Creator* and we are his image-bearing *creatures*, there is certainly a difference between God's memory and our own. In fact, God's memory is qualitatively different from ours. But there are similarities that reflect the image-bearing nature of our own power of remembrance, and these similarities, woven all through the fabric of Scripture, enable us to speak truthfully about God's memory.

God's memory, as God himself, is *eternal*. God remembers eternity as well as time. There is nothing in the divine trinitarian being that escapes the storehouse of God's memory. All of eternity is remembered. Neither is there anything in human history that is not caught by the seine-net of God's mind.[2] Every flapping and fleeting movement in the world is there, preserved. Whatever happens in the future will also be there. The Trinity never forgets.

God's memory is also *perfect*. Everything in God's memory is faithfully preserved, down to the last detail. God remembers not just the act of making a covenant with Noah, but the look of Noah's face when God spoke, the posture of his body bent in prayer, the curvature of every hair in his beard, the impression left in the ground where he knelt. Nothing, I say again, escapes the seine-net of God's mind.

Now, what does God do with these memories? We cannot say very much about this. Perhaps the divine persons speak about their shared memories amongst themselves. After all, "John 1 presents us with the reality of eternal divine speaking in the being of the Trinity."[3] At least, Scripture reveals that God *acts* based on his memory. The references to God's remembrance of the covenant with the patriarchs serve as the grounds upon which he acts to save and preserve his people.

Whatever else we might say in biblical speculation, we must affirm that God's memories are *precious* to him. Memories matter. They have a home in God's mind as long as he chooses to keep them there. He can, to the praise of his glorious grace, choose to forget our transgressions (Isa 43:25; Jer 31:34; Ezek 33:16; Heb 8:12; 10:17) when we repent and find our Spirit-forged identity in Jesus Christ. But nothing in Scripture suggests that anything else will be forgotten.

This means that Isaac's giggle has a home in the memory of God. God will forever recall the laugh that tumbled through his smile on that September night in 2017. Isaac's giggle will *never* be lost and gone forever. It is precious to God, and so he keeps it. The sorrow that my wife and I felt at the thought of one day not hearing that four-year-old laugh was real, but it is not irreversible. We felt sorrow at the passing of time. We felt as if life was comprised of bits of experience that were slipping through our finite fingers. *But it is*

---

2. I take this image from a poem by Robinson Jeffers, "The Purse-Seine."

3. Poythress, *God-Centered Biblical Interpretation*, 36.

*not.* We did not in that moment remember the infinite God, even as he ever remembers us.

Hearing your children laugh can reveal much about the character of God and his deep love for creation, as can a thousand other wonderful experiences that seem to slip away. The joy and goodness of all that we experience in God's grace will never ultimately fade. The intricate threads of conversation with my wife, the sound of my two-year-old daughter's voice when she calls to be taken out of her crib on Saturday mornings, the smell of fresh cut grass in the heat of summer, the taste of chocolate, Isaac's giggle—these things are not ships disappearing over the horizon of experience. They are not lost and gone forever. They live on in the eternal, perfect memory of the triune God.

The irony in this, of course, is that we remember so little and so infrequently—not just in terms of our experience but in terms of our greatest love: God himself. I stopped that night to store Isaac's giggle in my memory and to ruminate, with unbiblical melancholy, over the passing of time. But what about my memories of God? What about my memories of what he has done in my life and heart, and my memories of his word? What about the memories of pure, sacrificial, unyielding love from a God who chooses to forget my daily doubt and failure? What about memories of grace?

We all have the power to remember and the power to forget. We go through much of life focusing only on ourselves. We tend to lose sight of God's own memory, and that is a travesty, but it is a travesty that God has long suffered in his mercy and grace. He knows how prone we are to forget the past—both its weight and its beauty, the granite and the gold. But he has a history of gathering what we leave behind. He holds the precious things of time in eternity, the simple and the complex, the giggles and the gratitude. I lay my soul down to rest in that truth: The Trinity never forgets.

# 3

## "Good Morning"

STRANGE, HOW WE PROMENADE so thoughtlessly through the divine presence of God. In him, "we live, and move, and have our being" (Acts 17:28).[1] God is not just our Lord; he is our very atmosphere. Every day we awake to a world that is saturated with God's presence. God is here. He is among us. For me, nowhere is this more apparent and more striking than in our use of language.

I have said "Good morning" hundreds of thousands of times. Only now, after years of studying the nature of the Trinity and human communication, are my eyes opened to the depth of those two little words.[2]

"Good morning" is, of course, a greeting, which makes us downplay just how miraculous it is. When I utter it to my wife, I am opening the door of dialogue. I am emerging from the silence of my own soul and asking her to enter in. Language is the key to communion. It is *communion behavior*, a call to connect my heart

1. It is good to remember that this quotation comes from a Cretan philosopher, whom Paul quoted while in Athens. Even those outside the borders of God's covenant people were able to see, by God's common grace, that he alone was their reason for existence.

2. I did my ThM thesis at Westminster on the nature of language and its relation to the Trinity, which has now been published as *The Trinity, Language, and Human Behavior: A Reformed Exposition of the Language Theory of Kenneth L. Pike*, Reformed Academic Dissertations (Phillipsburg, NJ: P&R, 2018). Shortly after I finished this, I wrote a book on the centrality of language to all of life, entitled *The Speaking Trinity & His Worded World: Why Language Is at the Center of Everything*, forthcoming from Wipf & Stock.

and mind with those of another.[3] The miracle lies in the meeting: that two separate creatures could actually draw closer to one another, even amidst the swells of inner turmoil, the distractions and desires that make us so self-centered. Even in the storms of self-obsession, we can open our mouths and utter a bridge that brings us to someone else. The miraculous nature of this simple daily phenomenon goes back to God himself.

Our very first conversation partner, we often forget, was God (Gen 1:28–30; 2:16–17). God spoke to us. The eternal, unchangeable, omniscient, omnipresent God spoke intelligibly and clearly to finite creatures. How easy it is to gloss over that biblical fact! But it is nothing short of miraculous. We think of the Incarnation as a miraculous event, but the Incarnation was long preceded by the tiny reflections of this momentous event in God's own speech to us. As a friend reminded me recently, "When God first utters a particular word to a human being, his act is no more incredible than that most incredible act, the Incarnation."[4]

Let us ruminate on this a bit more. The eternal Son of God is described by John as *the Word* (John 1:1). Later in John's Gospel, Jesus calls himself *the truth* (John 14:6). As the true and eternal Word of God the Father, uttered forever in the power of the Holy Spirit, the Son of God is the original speech upon which God's speech to creatures is based.[5] Now, the Son would one day come as Immanuel, God with us, at the Incarnation. *But every time we see God utter a word before that moment, we have tiny reflections of the Incarnation.* The particular words that God speaks to his creatures, recorded in Scripture, are instances in which the infinite enters into the finite. When God speaks words to us, they do not then cease to be divine; they are still *God's* words, but they have taken on flesh in our world.[6]

---

3. I have written in more depth about this in "Closing the Gaps: Perichoresis and the Nature of Language," 299–322 and "Words for Communion," 5–8.

4. Poythress, *God-Centered Biblical Interpretation*, 33.

5. See Poythress, "God and Language."

6. K. Scott Oliphint's chapter on the mystery of the Incarnation is a helpful reminder of this wondrous truth. See *The Majesty of Mystery*, 54–79.

So all of God's speech is miraculous. All of God's speech to us is incarnational, and thus mysterious in a way that parallels the deeply mysterious union of the divine and human natures in the one person of Christ. In this light, it is indeed miraculous when God himself calls the very first morning "Good" (Gen 1:3, 18)!

The incarnational nature of God's speech to us lies behind our utterance of a casual greeting such as "Good morning," for we are made in the image of God (Gen. 1:26). Part of that image—in fact, what I believe is the core of the image—is our ability to communicate, our ability to speak.[7] When we say, "Good morning," we are echoing and imaging the God who called the very first morning "Good." Our speech, of course, is not miraculous in the sense that God's speech is, but this should not take away from the majesty and beauty of our daily dialogue. With every word we utter, we point to the glorious, personal Lordship of the God who speaks.[8]

But "Good morning" is miraculous in still other ways. Because we are image bearers of the God who speaks, we should expect that language is riddled with reflections of God's trinitarian nature. And it is.

One of the ways we see the Trinity in our speech is through a triad that the Christian linguist Kenneth Pike called *contrast*, *variation*, and *distribution*.[9] That language might seem technical, but it is really quite simple. "Good morning" is an utterance that *contrasts* with other utterances in its structure and sound. "Hey," "Hello," and "Hi" are other greetings that we could utter in the morning, each fulfilling a similar purpose. Whenever I speak the words "Good morning," they are slightly different from all of my other utterances of the same greeting. Perhaps I shorten some of

7. As Geerhardus Vos put it, "That man bears God's image means much more than that he is spirit and possesses understanding, will, etc. It means above all that he is disposed for communion with God, that all the capacities of his soul can act in a way that corresponds to their destiny only if they rest in God." Vos, *Anthropology*, 13.

8. For a fuller treatment of how language serves as evidence for God's existence, see Hibbs, "Imaging Communion," 35–51.

9. See the chapters corresponding to contrast, variation, and distribution in Pike, *Linguistic Concepts*.

the sounds ("G' morning"), or take more time to articulate them, or alter the intonation or volume of my voice. Whatever the difference might be, no matter how slight, each time I utter the greeting, it is a new *variation*, a unique physical manifestation of the same saying. Lastly, my words are always *distributed* in contexts. For instance, my "Good morning" must be uttered before 12:00pm. My words are also distributed in a string of dialogue, related to what has come before them and what will come after them. Perhaps they mark the beginning of a new conversation and signal the end of a previous one (with another person). We could go on and get into more details, but the general point is clear enough: every one of our utterances has *contrast*, *variation*, and *distribution*. These features interlock with each other. They are distinctly and simultaneously present in every utterance.

This triad of features goes all the way back to God himself.[10] The contrastive feature is derived from the Father, the variation feature from the Son, and the distribution feature from the Spirit. The Father is *contrasted* with false gods by Jesus in John 17:3. As he prays to the Father, Jesus calls him "the only true God." The Father, as God, is unique. There is none like him (Exod 8:10; Ps 113:5). The Son is the manifestation of the divine essence and perfect image of the Father, for Christ tells his disciples, "Whoever has seen me has seen the Father" (John 14:9). He is the eternal *variant* of the one divine essence. Lastly, the Spirit is the divine *context* (distribution) for the Father and the Son. The Father and the Son share their love for one another in the Spirit, for the Spirit belongs to both of them just as they belong to one another. The Spirit is of the Father (Matt 10:20) and of the Son (Rom 8:9). Another way of putting this is to say that the Spirit is the context of the love of the Father for the Son and the Son for the Father and the Holy Spirit for both. These three persons are one and indwell one another.

All of this stands behind the two-word greeting we use almost every day. But the most breath-taking sense of God's divine presence in language can be found in a metaphor. In uttering words,

---

10. For a discussion of how these features are governed by God in human language, see Poythress, *In the Beginning Was the Word*, 154–58.

we fail to see that we are, in a sense, words that God himself has uttered.[11] We are, as one theologian put it, "incorporated words, made to know God the Father through the Son and, through words, to be united with the Word of the Father."[12]

The Son is the eternal Word of the Father (John 1:1). He is the everlasting Son of God, but Adam is also referred to as the son of God (Luke 3:38), as is his progeny (Hos 11:1). Given the connection between God's eternal Son and his created sons and daughters, we have biblical warrant to consider ourselves words of our heavenly Father. We are creaturely words of God, uttered by the Father, shaped to the sound-image of Christ (Rom 8:29), sustained by his life-giving breath (Gen 2:7; Job 33:4).[13] We are living words: complex messages that God has uttered into being and shepherded through an atmosphere of time and space.

The natural question is, "As words, what do we *mean*?" Here is the greatest question of semantics we could ever ask, and we must ask it continually. We mean many things, but our most important meaning is found in our response to the saving word of God. As creaturely words of the Father, we find our meaning in response to the eternal Word of the Father come in the flesh. We are who we are only in dialogue with the Trinity. Our meaning, in this sense, is our value to God as men and women in Christ who are being used, in a host of different ways, to accomplish the purposes that he has set out for us. Our *meaning* as words of God includes our complex and contextual function in his eternal plan. This includes both our earthly life and our eternal communion with God. Our meaning is anchored in the fact that we are image bearers of God. The highest love God can have is love for himself, since he is the most worthy of such love. But in close second is the love he has for those who are made in his likeness. So, our meaning as words that bear the likeness of God is our response to God's eternal Word, a

11. Part of my inspiration for this idea comes from Pike, *Language in Relation to a Unified Theory of the Structure of Human Behavior*, 655–58.

12. Stăniloae, *The Holy Trinity*, 34.

13. I take the term "sound image" from Saussure, *Course in General Linguistics*.

response that is solely the work of the Holy Spirit. There is mysterious circularity here: that words find meaning in the Word as they are enlivened by the Spirit who eternally empowered that Word. We are encompassed on all sides by the divine speech of God. As I said at the outset, *in God* we live and move and have our being (Acts 17:28).

We can expand on this, somewhat playfully, to look at the larger chunks of our lives. We are words that God has spoken and upholds each day, and yet each day can be understood metaphorically as a sentence: a syntactical string of structurally related events, unified and integrated according to God's will and purpose. A week is a paragraph, a month a discussion, a year a chapter, a decade a book, a life a library. The narrative of time unfolds alongside the narrative of fulfilled personal meaning as we grow in our relationship with God. What speech we are! What a worded world we live in! I think of this often and find that expressing it poetically helps me to worship God.

> One Voice, one Word, one Breath:
>
> God said himself into a void.
>
> From holy speech came water and wind,
>
> light and fire, feathers and fur, scales and skin.
>
> And then he spoke his likeness:
>
> Echoing words that work and play,
>
> Echoing words that speak and *mean* in dialogue
>
> With one Voice, one Word, one Breath.

I said at the outset, it is strange that we promenade so thoughtlessly through the divine presence of God. God is present in language. The beating heart of the Trinity is thumping underneath every human word, no matter how trivial or commonplace. "Good morning," as it turns out, is much more than a greeting. It has imbedded within it the deepest secret of the universe and the nature of God himself.

# 4

## Dust at Daybreak

THE WORLD OF WATER seems strange and beautiful to us. That fish float through an atmosphere holding their movement in grace, that sea grass sways and turns underwater as if dancing to soft music, that sediment and stones wander and skip through a current, carefree as children—these things are mesmerizing.

We need something to remind us that we live in an atmosphere not so far removed from this. Water and ether may seem worlds apart, but they are two regions of the same world that God spoke into being. In fact, it was through God's very speech that these regions were separated (Gen 1:6). We might gaze in adoration at the movement of fish and think of God's unparalleled creativity, but what about the smaller things right before our eyes? Do they evoke worship in us?

They should, but we are often ignorant of them, distracted by what seem to be "greater" things. But I have found that some of the greatest testaments to God's Lordship and presence are very small, even as small as a particle of dust.

I always wake up early to read and write. One summer morning, I came downstairs in the dark silence, opened the blinds in our living room, made some coffee, and then sat down on the couch with my book. I was engrossed in the reading until the dawn broke and began spilling soft, orange light through the windows. I picked up my head after writing down a note and found that the living room was a glorious, awe-inspiring atmosphere. Dust particles, carpet fibers, and dog hair were drifting and dancing on tiny thermals—hundreds, thousands of them rising and falling, spinning in the light. I felt as if I were underwater, watching currents play with particles in a way that reflected the winsome harmony I could only attribute to God.

I wrote a poem about a similar experience I had on a December afternoon.[1]

### God of Dust

Early afternoon in late December:
Clouds covering the face of the sun
Parted and let light flood the living room,
A current picking up carpet fibers and dog hair,
Offering them up on tiny thermals,
An ordinary sacrifice
From time to eternity.
One small dust particle dances,
Pirouettes, waltzes, sighs,
And descends, drifting back
Into the blue and white carpet.
This—that is what you tell them.
This is why I believe.

God's Lordship and detailed governance of the smallest things does not attract our attention enough. Perhaps this is because we feel as if the world is mute, an impersonal planet spinning on an impersonal axis in an impersonal universe. But the world is not *just there*. As we noted earlier, everything that exists does so in the environment of God: "in him we live and move and have our being" (Acts 17:28).

The world is not just *of* God; it is *in* God. This does not mean that the world is divine. Rather, it means that every element of the world *relies on* God for its existence. More specifically, it relies on God's speech. The writer of Hebrews tells us that God "upholds the universe by the word of his power" (Heb 1:3). The speech of God

---

1. This poem was originally published in the July/August 2016 issue of *Perspectives: A Journal of Reformed Thought*.

holds the world up.[2] And because God is present in his speech, we should expect every part of the world to reveal something about him, even dust particles.[3]

Another way of putting this is to say that the world "speaks" to us in the sense that it reveals the trinitarian God who made it.[4] Augustine reflected on this in his *Confessions*: "I love you, Lord, with no doubtful mind but with absolute certainty. You pierced my heart with your word, and I fell in love with you. But the sky and the earth too, and everything in them—all these things around me are telling me that I should love you; and since they never cease to proclaim this to everyone, those who do not hear are left without excuse."[5] The sky and earth, the wind and the dust, tell us of God.

Of course, the question we will have (and should have) every time we consider this in a given situation is obvious: What is *this* telling me about God? Let us have some fun with this question in the context of dust particles.[6]

First, every dust particle that I see floating through the air is a *unit*, a thing. Part of the glory of my summer morning scene lay in the fact that many distinct particles were drifting through the same space. Each particle was its own, unique. Each was *original*, we might say. Each one was also stable. None of the dust particles spontaneously broke apart. Each was held together in a way that preserved its singularity. I found joy in that singularity: a dog's hair slightly curved in on itself, a carpet fiber with two subtle waves

2. Poythress, *Redeeming Science*, 37–44.

3. On God being present in his speech, see Frame, *The Doctrine of the Word of God*, 63–68.

4. "But in addition to speaking in the Bible, God speaks in all created things (Psalm 19) and through our own human constitution (e.g., Rom 1:32). His word is truly inescapable." Poythress, "God's Lordship in Interpretation," 32.

5. Saint Augustine, *Confessions* 10.8.

6. In the following discussion, I am using the three perspectives introduced by Kenneth Pike: particle, wave, and field. See Pike, *Linguistic Concepts*, 19–38. I am also leaning on Poythress' concepts of *originary, manifestational,* and *concurrent* with reference to God's presence. See Poythress, *God-Centered Biblical Interpretation*, 36–41. These concepts are related to Kenneth Pike's language theory, especially *contrast, variation,* and *distribution.*

in it, a speck of house dust falling from the corner of the dresser where our television sits. I found joy in the uniqueness and stability of every tiny particle.

I also found joy in their *waves* of movement. Their movement is what made me feel as if I were underwater, watching them drift slowly within churning currents of air. The whole scene was dynamic. It was not just dust particles frozen in space; their movement was what drew me to them. Their rising and falling, turning and twisting—it had an almost hypnotic effect on me. I was caught up in the movement with them. I was watching not just units, but units in motion.

Lastly, I found joy in their intersections, their crossing paths, their multilayered spatial *relationships*. Seeing all of these fibers and particles drifting in the air was breathtaking because the intricate network of their movement was controlled by the speech of God, every subtle shift in direction, even those caused by the shallow breaths I was taking as I gazed in wonder. I was awestruck not just by units in motion, but by moving pieces in relationship.

All of these features were present simultaneously: the units, the motion, and the relationships. They were part of the one mesmerizing experience that I took in from the couch. But what does any of this have to do with God?

Stable units such as dust particles must derive their stability from something, or someone. Secular worldviews would have us attribute the stable nature of the dust particles to their physical makeup or their molecular structure. In other words, they will point to principles to explain the stability of units in the world. But that is not really an explanation. Explanations are only real if they come from *persons*, not from principles. Principles are explanatory, no doubt, but persons must stand behind the principles or else the principles are ultimately unstable and capricious, which means they are not really principles at all.

The way I see it, the person of the *Father* is behind the stability of those tiny dust particles. Their stability is a temporal derivative of his eternal stability. James describes the first person of the Godhead as the "Father of lights, with whom there is no variation or shadow due to change" (James 1:17). The Father is eternally unbegotten, supremely stable, utterly immoveable. Because the Father created the world (with the Son and Spirit), we are bound to find pieces of reality all over the place that reflect his unchangeable nature on a creaturely level. When we see the dust particles as stable units, we are seeing a quality that is derived from the *person* who created them. The art reflects the artist.

The person of the *Son* is behind the movement of the particles. The Son is the eternal dynamism of God, ever begotten from the Father, bound to him in love through the Spirit, and carrying out his behest as the all-powerful *Word*. This applies to creation, certainly: "By the word of the Lord the heavens were made, and by the breath of his mouth all their host" (Ps 33:6). But it also applies to the Father's continuing governance of the world. The prophet Isaiah records God's own statement of this divine fact:

> For as the rain and the snow come down from heaven
> and do not return there but water the earth,
> making it bring forth and sprout,
> giving seed to the sower and bread to the eater,
> so shall my word be that goes out from my mouth;
> it shall not return to me empty,
> but it shall accomplish that which I purpose,
> and shall succeed in the thing for which I sent it.
> (Isa 55:10–11)

The Son, as the Word of his Father (John 1:1), is ever active, always moving to control the marvelous panoply of creation. The dust particles moving through the air derive their dynamism from him. *They* move ultimately because *he* moves. When we see the dust particles drifting through the air, we are seeing a quality that is derived from the *person* who created them. Again, the art reflects the artist.

Lastly, the Spirit, as he who proceeds from the Father and the Son, is the relational context for the love of the Father for the Son and the Son for the Father. The Holy Spirit is the person who grounds the divine interrelations. In the Spirit, the Father and the Son eternally dwell and interpenetrate one another. The relationships that we find in the created world are derived from him. There are earthly relationships because, in the Spirit, there is divine relationship. When we see the dust particles in their interrelations, in their multilayered networks, drifting through the air, we are seeing a quality that is derived from the *person* who created them. Once more, the art reflects the artist.

Now, the three persons are one God. We cannot tear the Father from the Son, or the Spirit from the Son, or the Father from the Spirit because they share the same essence. The three persons of the Godhead are essentially one and yet personally distinct. Our God is one and three. Each person exhaustively represents the other two.[7] Analogously, we cannot observe parts of the world in which stability, dynamism, and relationships are *not* present and coinherent.

So, what do dust particles tell us about God? Quite a bit. I looked at the dust that morning and saw a three-personed God who is stable, active, and relational. I saw a God who is reflected even in the miniscule. We try to wipe dust away with cloth and cleaner. Sometimes we would be better off just blowing on it and watching it testify to the Trinity.

7. Van Til, *A Survey of Christian Epistemology*, 78.

# 5

## Shadows on the Grass

DARKNESS HAS A POOR reputation among Christians. There are scads of texts in the Bible that use darkness as a symbol for evil and punishment (Deut 28:29; 1 Sam 2:9; 2 Sam 22:29; Job 17:13; 19:8; 20:26; 24:17; 30:26; 38:19; Pss 18:28; 82:5; 88:18; 143:3; Prov 2:13; 4:19; Eccl 2:14; 5:17; Isa 5:30; 8:22; Lam 3:2; Ezek 32:8; Joel 2:31; Amos 5:20; Matt 6:23; 8:12; 22:13; 25:30; Luke 11:34; 22:53; John 1:5; 3:19; 8:12; 12:46; Rom 2:19; 13:12; 2 Cor 6:14; Eph 5:8,11; 6:12; Col 1:13; 1 Thess 5:4; 1 Pet 2:9; 2 Pet 2:4,17; 1 John 1:5–6; 2:8–11; Rev 16:10). The poor reputation of darkness is thus warranted, especially given that evil is rebellion against the Father of *lights* (James 1:17).

But not all texts in Scripture speak of darkness as evil. At the dawn of creation, in fact, darkness is not associated with a serpent, nor does it signal impending judgment or death. Instead, it is portrayed as a stage, an arena in which creation unfolds.

It has always been fascinating to me that there are only two things in Genesis 1 that are not *explicitly* discussed as creations of God: water and darkness (Gen 1:2). These elements seem to have been there before the other parts of the created order came about. Now, by good and necessary consequence, we know that God did, in fact, create these things. And if darkness was part of a creation originally deemed "good" by God (Gen 1:31), then is there not room for us to find a positive side to darkness?

Perhaps Rainer Maria Rilke goes a bit further than this in his verse:

> You, darkness, of whom I am born—
>
> I love you more than the flame
> that limits the world
> to the circle it illumines
> and excludes all the rest.
>
> But the dark embraces everything:
> shapes and shadows, creatures and me,
> people, nations—just as they are.
>
> It lets me imagine
> a great presence stirring beside me.
>
> I believe in the night.[1]

It seems doubtful that Rilke had in mind any of the Scripture passages listed above when he wrote the poem. Still, there is something encouraging about it that is not, I believe, altogether foreign to Scripture.

I remember the very first time I read this poem. I have struggled with an anxiety disorder for over a decade. When I first read Rilke, I was dealing with a strong swell of anxiety that came whenever I had to drive at night. The night seemed threatening to me—isolating and exclusive (the very opposite view that Rilke presents). I despised the night. The pale gray sky at dusk pushed forward black skeletons of trees in a way that made my soul feel cold, sick, and helpless. When the night came, I wanted to hide in the light. But that is no way to live.

That is why Rilke's verse struck me so deeply. The last line, in particular, has never left my mind: "I believe in the night." It is difficult to say exactly what he means by it. The context of the poem suggests that he is praising the night, and so "the night" might very well have been the object of his faith. But the way I always read it

---

1. *Rilke's Book of Hours: Love Poems to God*, 62–63.

was to view the night as the arena in which belief comes to maturity. "During the night—*that* is when I believe." Darkness is the context for light, the setting for the certainty of faith. In that sense, it is not unequivocally evil. Rather, God *uses* darkness, just as he uses all other elements of creation, for his own good purposes.

A case in point is the presence of shadows. Some weeks ago, I was sitting outside on the bench in our backyard, reading a book. I liked the way the natural light of the sun struck the pages, illuminating their slightly textured surface. Electric light seems to shout at pages, demanding they surrender their meaning. Sunlight, on the other hand, carries on a whispered conversation with the ink and pulp. Books seem more contented in the sun.

I looked up from one of these pages and saw the shadows of willow branches dancing on the grass. As the wind blew, the darker shadows of the tree limbs rose and fell, and the thin leaves of the threaded branches cast a lighter shadow around them. I looked up at the sun and thought about how much peace I was finding simply in watching shadows. I had the sun to thank for that, or rather the God who made the sun to rule over the day.

I began thinking about the nature of shadows. Shadows are derivatives; they are entirely dependent on something else for their existence. The shadows I was watching were dependent on the willow tree. Some ninety million miles away, in the dark silence of space, the sun was casting its light toward the earth. That light confronted an obstacle in a little town in Pennsylvania, on a street called Park Avenue. On that street, was a house with a backyard. In that backyard was a willow tree. As the light met that tree, it could not pass through it, so it went around it, tracing the trunk, the limbs, and thousands of tiny leaves. The result of this tracing was a shadow, a complex and dynamic replica of the willow tree. That replica could not exist without the original. Remove the tree, and you remove the shadow. The dependence of the shadow on the original object drew my attention to the idea in Genesis 1 and the idea from Rilke's poem: Darkness is a context for light.

But then I paused. As I looked at the shadows waving on the grass, I realized I had gotten it backwards. The darkness was not a context for the light; the light was a context for the darkness. Without the sun, there would be no shadows in the first place. Without the God who is a light unto himself (1 John 1:5), there is no such thing as darkness.[2] When Genesis 1:2 says, "darkness was over the face of the deep," we overlook the fact that for such darkness to exist, there had to be light already present. *Darkness always presupposes light.*

In our world, it seems as if darkness is a context for light, but in reality the Father of lights (James 1:17) is the context for everything else, darkness included. First John 1:5 says, "God is light, and in him is no darkness at all." This does not mean that darkness is unequivocally evil, but it does mean that darkness is *always* used by God for greater purposes than we can fathom. Even in its most potent forms, darkness (whether literal or metaphorical) is a servant of light. When Rilke says that the darkness "embraces everything," he may have overlooked this truth: Darkness can embrace everything only because light has embraced it first.

This brings renewed meaning to Jesus' words, "I am the light of the world" (John 8:12). It makes perfect sense for the second person of the Trinity, who created all things, to claim himself as the light. His Father is light, and he is in his Father (John 14:11). And when John writes in the Prologue to his gospel, "The light shines in the darkness, and the darkness has not overcome it" (John 1:5), we can say in affirmation, "Of course it didn't! Darkness cannot overcome the very person who created it and gave it a context for existence." No piece of art has the power to overcome its artist.

So, shadows are derivative. They are replicas of originals. But darkness itself is derivative because it is entirely dependent on the God of light. Apart from him, darkness would cease to be. While I mentioned earlier that darkness is the setting for the certainty of faith, that is not the whole truth of the matter. While darkness is an arena for the light of faith, it is the Lord of light himself that

2. I follow others who affirm that God is a light unto himself. The light that he creates first is not earthly light, but a kind of self-referential light on the basis of which he creates earthly light. See Waltke, *Genesis*, 61; Milgrom, "The Alleged 'Hidden Light,'" 44; and Smith, "Light in Genesis 1:3," 1:127–31.

brings our feeble faith to fruition. God alone is responsible for our burgeoning faith in a dark world.

Let us end with the shadows on the grass. The shadows from the willow tree ultimately point to the dependence of darkness on light. God uses the darkness for his greater purposes. He was using the shadows of the willow tree to turn my eyes not towards the light of the sun, but towards the light of himself. Shadows have as much to say about God as anything else in our world. When you see a shadow, remember that it is only there because it depends on the light of the sun, but the light of the sun depends upon the original light, God himself. Shadows dancing on the grass are thus reminders of the God who burns brightly, and whose brightness is the context for all that is lesser than himself.

Perhaps we could write a new poem in response to Rilke's verse.

> You, light, of whom I am born—
>
> I love the way you enflame the world,
> burning behind the sun
> that allows for the shadows
> that dance on the ground.
>
> Darkness is but a response to you,
> a child stepping out in front of his parent.
> And you turn him back toward yourself,
> saying, "Follow my lead."
>
> You, my light, embrace all:
> dust and darkness, tree leaves and daylight.
> Nothing can be mute before you—
> All must respond and speak.
>
> You let me see
> a light greater than all light,
> burning around, behind, and within.
>
> I believe in the God who illumines.

# 6

## A Crouton for a Croissant

WE LIVE IN A world where words are thrown about like well-worn pennies—stained and faded from neglect, covered in the filth that accrues from careless exchange. Perhaps it has always been this way since the fall. We seldom pause to think about the deeper meanings of the words we use and their relationships to the rest of our lives—not to mention their relationship to what God is doing. Nor do we think about the deeper meaning of our mistakes in speech.

Consider that word, "mistake," in the context of a child's use of language. This morning, my two-year-old daughter, Nora, pointed to her breakfast plate and said, "No—I don't wanna crouton." She was pointing, however, at a croissant. I opened my mouth to correct her but then closed it again. "Okay, sweetie. You don't have to eat a crouton."

I did not correct her because I didn't *want* to. Her speech was precious to me; it was a fleeting gift that time would soon unwrap and set at the foot of a mountain of other memories. Before it went to the mountain, I wanted to hold it my heart. I wanted to enjoy her speech for just a moment, before we got to an era in which correcting her would be commonplace. I wanted to cherish a quiet sense of awe—an awe not at the use of words, but at their misuse.

Our son, Isaac, once had a vocabulary that bore little resemblance to modern English. He made up sounds as best he could to mimic those he heard his parents making. "Mnamna" was "tomato"; "Clu-culah" was "clementine"; "boomba" was "ball." Not once did I correct him. Quite the opposite: part of me wishes he still spoke that way.

These "mistakes" that my children have made in speech fill me with a sense of awe because they are precious and personal markers of *growth*. Nora now knows what a croissant is as compared to a crouton. Isaac no longer asks to throw a boomba with his daddy. These are now relics, fingerprints on the wall of their linguistic history, painted over and nearly forgotten. But I will not forget; I will remember. As their father, I will always find deep joy in watching them develop, even in the details of their speech. Such "mistakes" are and always will be magical to me. They demand remembrance because *growth* is one of the dearest elements of this world. Dear to us, yes, but dear also to the three-personed God.

The Trinity, after all, was first a gardener. "And the Lord God planted a garden in Eden, in the east, and there he put the man whom he had formed" (Gen 2:8). I sometimes playfully speculate as to how this scene unfolded: The Father uttering his Son in the power of the Spirit as blades of grass rose to attention, fiddleheads of ferns unfurled, tree roots gripped and burrowed into the black soil, and sunflowers sprouted to open their great crowns in worship. A world rich with color and life climbing towards the sun that God had spoken into the sky . . . . Oh yes, long before sin stained the world, God loved growth. The first humans were meant to be mimetic gardeners, working the land and tending to the plants and trees (Gen 2:15). They were meant to be gardeners after God's own heart (1 Sam 13:14).

After the fall, God took up his love for growth in *us* through his plan of redemption. We are rosebushes infiltrated with weeds and bramble, saplings sagging from lack of water, perennials longing for paradise. In a thousand ways, *we* became God's garden, desperately in need of divine tending for any hope of salvation. And so the Trinity tended us, at great cost.

Perhaps the most profound love of growth in our redemption is shown in God's mercy and grace. Mercy (not getting what you deserve) and grace (getting what you do not deserve) are not actions taken without a context. Rather, they are actions of God in the context of our spiritual *growth*.

God first shows mercy when he does not bring immediate judgment on Adam and Eve for their violation of his command. Their eating of the forbidden fruit warranted a swift death penalty, for he told them, "in the day that you eat of it you shall surely die" (Gen 2:17). But God delayed this. They did not die that day. God granted them continued life, and that is great mercy. Why did God do this? The rest of God's actions in Scripture suggest that the answer lies in God's love for us (John 3:16; Rom 5:8), a love that wills our *growth* in Christlikeness. Adam and Eve would live many more years, difficult years, years full of pain and toil. That was their punishment. But their years would also be filled with experiences that drew them closer to the God they worshiped. Every mistake they made following their first grand mistake would be an opportunity for God to grow them, to tend them. Every harsh word repented of would be a weed plucked from the soil of their heart by divine hands. Every sense of bitterness, every thoughtless action, every selfish decision—these would be opportunities for growth, times for divine tending. God would grow the garden of his people through their mistakes. In that sense, Mary was not so far off when she mistook the risen Son of God for a gardener (John 20:15). The triune God *is* a gardener, the greatest gardener. He has and always will use our mistakes as opportunities to conform us to the image of his Son (Rom 8:29). By the power of the Holy Spirit working in us, our mistakes, tolerated in God's mercy, are converted to opportunities for growth.

God does the same through his grace, even in ways that we might not perceive as gracious. Many people might consider God's expulsion of Adam and Eve from the garden as harsh. Did he really need to go so far as to bar them from the tree of life (Gen 3:22)? Could God not simply have forgiven them? God's expulsion of Adam and Eve, his keeping them from the tree of life, was actually an act of grace. Had Adam and Eve eaten from the tree of life, they would have acted in sin and been preserved in their corruption forever. They would have "taken [eternal life] by their own effort rather than by receiving it by God's grace. . . . God's intention is to give them eternal life in his own way, not through their grasping but through his grace, in the cross of Jesus."[1] Turning them away from the garden, then, was an act of grace, propelling them and their progeny to receive an even greater grace in the gift of Jesus Christ. As with God's mercy, God's grace would pave the way for personal growth. Grace would lead to repentance (Rom. 2:4). Grace would lead to growth.

God's mercy and grace were preparatory for personal growth, a growth for which he is solely responsible. This is deeply mysterious—that in the midst of our sin and rebellion God would pour out his love for us, working our redemption through intermittent and frequently stunted growth in Christlikeness. But Scripture tells us that this was precisely what God intended to do because of his *love* for us. Paul writes in Romans 5:8, "God shows his love for us in that while we were still sinners, Christ died for us." While we were still sinners, while we were still in the process of growing into Christ (and very far from perfection), while we were still making a thousand mistakes a day—*that* is when Christ died for us. Christ died for us *as we were growing*, knowing that the Holy Spirit would work in us to produce only what God himself could bring to fruition (1 Cor 3:7). Christ died for us in the midst of our growth, knowing that the Spirit would maintain our growth, and that the Father would complete it. So I say again: the Trinity is a gardener, a God in love with growth.

For some reason, we forget all of this when we see someone make a mistake. We judge, we evaluate, we speculate about motives. In our own lives, we strive for perfection and hope to avoid all possible mistakes. That attitude is not a bad one, since Jesus tells us to strive for perfection (Matt 5:48). But we seldom look at a mistake and ask, "How is God using this for growth?" It is perhaps easier to ask this question in harmless contexts, such as in my children's ongoing language development. We grow in our knowledge and use of language by making mistakes and hearing others correct us. But we should ask this question just as frequently

1. Frame, *Systematic Theology*, 855n16.

when it comes to the more serious mistakes we make. A Christian's mistakes are *never* victories for Satan. They might appear that way, but God's great governing providence makes all evil serve his good purposes. That means that every mistake, every error, every sin is a momentous occasion signaling God's governing growth. Mistakes are not just markers of our depravity. They are more than that. They are the triune God's spadework in the soil of the soul. They are opportunities for the great gardener to tend our lives and help us grow.

We should eagerly desire such growth. As plants in God's grand arbor, we should shake in the wind of the Spirit at the notion that the trinitarian Lord of all would come to tend our personal lives. John Newton's 1779 hymn put it eloquently:

> I asked the Lord that I might *grow*
> In faith, and love, and every grace;
> Might more of His salvation know,
> And seek, more earnestly, His face.

Asking the Lord to help us grow is simultaneously asking him to work through our mistakes to provide opportunities for growth.

This is not to say that we should embrace mistakes because they are positive in themselves (Rom 6:1). We all earnestly seek, by the Spirit's power, to image Christ and our heavenly Father with perfection (Matt 5:48). But in the striving for that perfection, we cannot forget God's love of growth. That is why, when I encounter the "mistakes" in my children's speech, I smile. They are quiet testaments to growth. I have no wish to rush past them. God has no wish to rush past *us*. He is patient beyond measure, and finds joy in our growth.

The next time you encounter a mistake, in your life or in someone else's, remember that the Trinity is standing by with a spade and pruning shears, ready to use our missteps for his own magnificence. God is our gardener. Our growth is close to his heart. Daily mistakes can be wonderful reminders of who God is and what he is doing.

# 7

## Dog Sleeping in the Sun

A DOG SLEEPING IN the sun is a wondrously peaceful still-life. Every weekend, our dog, Buckley, lays himself out on the couch, centering his body on a square of light pouring in through the window. I sometimes pause as I walk through the living room to watch his rib cage rise and fall, his shoulder joint lifting and lowering slightly toward his face and then away from it. Now and then he twitches his black whiskers, shifts his position, and settles back into the sunlight.

It is strangely comforting to fall asleep in the sun. While the rest of your environment hums and hustles—lawn mowers blaring, cars swishing by, children laughing, birds calling—you can lay your head down and be a still point in the turning world. It feels like stepping out of a stream for a bit, letting the water rush by before wading back into the current.

The best part, I find, is waking to the light. I know, it is unsettling because you feel more like an alien at first. You must claw your way back into the ordinary, and this takes discomforting effort. But in another sense, it gloriously reflects the way in which God burns behind the physical world, upholding and sustaining all that exists, even while much of existence—especially humanity—is not conscious of his presence. We are not often aware of God. But that does not keep him from being ever present. God is immanent despite our ignorance. The sun shines while we sleep.

Of course, we can see and feel the sun, which makes it easy to acknowledge. With God, it is different. God is a Spirit (Westminster Shorter Catechism, Q. 4). That simple fact means we cannot see him. And yet Scripture tells us that we can see revelation of God everywhere (Rom 1:18–21). That is perhaps one of the most profound paradoxes of the Christian faith: that a three-personed Spirit whom we cannot see "shows" himself to us everywhere in the works of his speech.

We can all too easily forget that latter point: God has created and sustains the world through divine speech. While we cannot see God, we can see the effects of his speech. We can see the work that has come from the words of the Speaker, but the Speaker remains beyond our comprehension, clothed in blinding light (Ps 104:2). Yet this does not mean that all we have are works from a divine wordsmith that float through time and space. For the speaking God binds his personal *presence* to his speech.[1] God is *with* his worded world. So, as I have said many times, we should expect that the products of God's speech are consequently marked with his presence.

This is reflected in our own use of speech, which images that of God. Take the word "light" in the sentence, "My dog fell asleep in the *light*." That word obviously refers to sunlight, physical light. At first glance, we might think that's all there is to it. But what *is* sunlight? The answers will vary, depending on whom you ask. A non-Christian would be content to say that the sun is merely a giant star, burning millions of miles away. As it burns, it produces heat and light waves that travel through space and time to our planet. Sunlight is the effect of a star, nothing more.

But for a Christian, who believes that God spoke that star into being, sunlight is much more than the effect of a star. This great star has a purpose that God established for it. And because it came from God's own personal speech, it reflects something of God's personal presence.

---

1. On God being present with his words, see Poythress, *In the Beginning Was the Word*, 26; Frame, *Doctrine of the Word of God*, 63–68.

It reflects the presence of his creativity. God chose to create the cosmos; his hand was not forced. In other words, God *willed* to create; he *wanted* to create. And at the dawn of time, God exercised this potent proclivity to manifest a world that reflected him at every turn. The triune God fused idea, energy, and power in forming the cosmos.[2] Thus, the stars were thoughts of the Father, brought to burn by the dynamism of the Son and in the power of the Holy Spirit. The stars are marks of trinitarian creativity. They are the realized thoughts of a sacred and holy artist. And because God created the stars to reflect him (since the whole natural world reflects him; Rom 1:20), there is a sense in which that reflection signals his presence. God left his watermark on every facet of the world because he is a God who desires to be *with* his people. When his people look at the things all around them, they are not meant to see brute objects. They are meant to see a world that testifies to the glory of its personal, triune maker (Ps 19:1–4). So, when we see the sunlight, we are not simply processing waves of heat and light. Rather, we are standing in the creativity of a God who wants us to know that he is here, that he is everywhere. The sun reflects the presence of a creative, personal God. We could reword the sentence "My dog fell asleep in the *light*" as "My dog fell asleep in the potent creativity of the God who is with us."

The sun also reflects God's stability. The sun sends forth its light with regularity, but it is not the original light. It does not rely on itself for its existence or on the happenstance of a world that exploded into motion. The artist behind the stars is God himself. In forming the stars, he expressed something of his own character, for "God is light" (1 John 1:5). "The ultimate anchorage for the word *light* is in God himself, who is light. God by his own character and faithfulness gives ultimate stability to meaning in this world."[3] So, not only is the sun a testament to God's stability, but even the word that I use to convey a part of this creation, *light*,

---

2. I am here following Dorothy Sayers's trinitarian view of the creator God, as reflected in *The Mind of the Maker*, 35–45.

3. Poythress, "God and Language," 104.

relies on the stability of God. We could reword the sentence "My dog fell asleep in the *light*" as "My dog fell asleep in God's stability."

Lastly, the sun reflects the presence of God's grace. We have done nothing to merit the sunlight. It pours through the window of our home only because God has purposed it to do so. The gospel of Jesus Christ, whom we gather to worship, is the climax of God's grace, not its inauguration. As the sun shines and the rain falls, we are reminded that God is a giver (Matt 5:45). He always has been. The sunlight is a testament to the continual presence of his grace. We could reword the sentence "My dog fell asleep in the *light*" as "My dog fell asleep in the grace of God."

Let us draw these threads together as we return to the image of a dog dozing in the daylight. Nothing in this world exists of itself. It is all dependent. When we see the light, we can draw our attention to the God behind it, the God who dwells eternally in light that is unapproachable (1 Tim 6:16). The sunlight cascading past the curtains and warming the black fur of my dog's body, light that wraps his whiskers and the curves of his ears, is a testament to God. It is a sign of God's presence, which surrounds and pervades every fiber of his creation as he moves it according to his will and purpose. God is *that* involved.

Do not mistake the sunlight for sunlight, or the trees for trees. Do not mistake wind for wind, or sound for sound. Do not mistake the ordinary for the ordinary. In this world, there is no such thing as the ordinary. God is present here. Everywhere we look are testaments to divine presence. God is the light behind the light, the one who burns and shines in self-communion. He is the wind behind the wind, the one who moves the world. He is the sound behind the sound, the one who speaks from eternity past. Our world is an animated echo of the Trinity. Everywhere is Father, Son, and Spirit. That is no ordinary world.

We do not think of this often. We might feel little need to do so. After all, the dog sleeps better knowing that he will wake to a world that is the same as the one he closed his eyes to. But we cannot lose the profundity of the ordinary. Dogs sleeping in the sun reveal much more than we might imagine. When we go on assuming that they are *just* dogs sleeping in the sun, we give up the real gold of godliness. For godliness is not bare behavior. It is behavior that flows from vision. The one who sees God in all things finds it unbearable to ignore banalities, for they are the glue binding God's world together, a world that is everywhere upheld by the Word of his power (Heb 1:3). Smile at the dog sleeping in the sun. He is resting in the beauty, power, and grace of God, as we all should.

# 8

## Wind in the Trees

It is autumn now, and I am frequently looking up. The sound of the leaves rustling in the wind changes slightly from the summer to the fall: the green leaves of summer are full of life, and their rubbing together makes a soft sound; the brown leaves of autumn are emptying of life, and their rubbing together makes a sharp sound. I love the sharpness, the way the leaves seem like a paper that God has fashioned in the canopy. I love to stare at the trees swaying in the wind, singing their papery song to any who would listen.

Karl Ove Knausgaard, a contemporary Scandinavian author, wrote a letter to his unborn daughter. It is a beautiful letter, reflecting his passion for life and his desire to share it with her. At one point in the letter, he writes with adoration, "The blood flowing through the veins, the grass growing in the soil, the trees, oh the trees swaying in the wind. These astounding things, which you will soon encounter and see for yourself, are so easy to lose sight of, and there are almost as many ways of doing that as there are people."[1] It is as easy for us to lose our sense of awe as it is to forget a dollar bill in our back pocket. And it is not just awe that we lose; we lose sight of the God who is present in the world. And that is no small thing, for "to know God is to know many things about his ways with the world."[2] Ignoring the wind in the trees is tantamount to ignoring what we might know about God.

1. Ove Knausgaard, *Autumn*, 5.
2. Poythress, *God-Centered Biblical Interpretation*, 137.

Wind, I have always found, is a wonderful testament to the Holy Spirit. Jesus once said, rather poetically, "The wind blows where it wishes, and you hear its sound, but you do not know where it comes from or where it goes. So it is with everyone who is born of the Spirit" (John 3:8). The Spirit is compared to the wind because we cannot see the paths of the wind, not before it reaches us nor after it moves beyond us. We see its effects. It calls and whistles; it carries the leaves. But we do not *know* where it has come from or where it is going. Its origin and end are beyond seeking out.

This seems to be a special sense in which the Holy Spirit is reflected in our world. The origin of the Spirit, as God, is eternal; we cannot explain it. We cannot *know* eternity. That is something privy only to God himself. So also, the Spirit's end is self-determined. We know God's end *for us*, that we will spend eternity in communion with him, but it is slightly different to say what God's end is for himself. That is not to imply that these two ends are in any way at odds with each other. It is simply to acknowledge that God is God, and we are not.

We do see something of the Spirit's origin and end in relation to us at the bookends of Scripture, but this is still profoundly mysterious. In Genesis 1:2, the Spirit is the breath of God hovering over the surface of the dark waters. There is no reference to where the Spirit has come from because the Spirit has come from God himself, and later revelation reveals that the Spirit is God. So, *God* was hovering over the surface of the waters. Why? We do not know. We are told only that the Spirit of God is present at creation. And that is something that should draw our attention: God is *present* with the world he has made. Pay close attention to the presence of God. He was *there*, and he is *here* (Job 38; Ps 139:7–12).

In Revelation, we find something similar regarding God's presence in the Spirit. After Jesus' divine identification in Revelation 22:16, we read, "The Spirit and the Bride say, 'Come.' And let the one who hears say, 'Come.' And let the one who is thirsty come; let the one who desires take the water of life without price" (Rev 22:17). Why does the Spirit say, "Come"? Certainly, as many theologians have noted, he is beckoning us into communion with the saints. But I find it odd that few comment on this as a marker of the Spirit's presence. This verse is, as Berkhof put it, a "beautiful invitation."[3] It is an invitation not just to commune with the saints but to commune with the Spirit of God himself. The Spirit is present at the dawn of time, but he is also present at the dawn of eternity. This presence is ultimately mysterious: we do not know where the Spirit has come from or where the Spirit is going because the Spirit is God himself, and God's ways are beyond searching out (Rom 11:33).

This does not mean that God is some divine vagrant, wandering around aimlessly in himself with no purpose. Rather, it means that it is not possible for limited, finite creatures to trace and explain his origins and ends. Some of them he reveals to us; others he does not. We struggle with this very much in our own lives, because what we do not understand seems either chaotic or irrational or both. But we let our limitation lead to lunacy when we assume that the all-powerful and all-purposeful God has origins and ends that we can fathom. If we could fathom them, then we would be divine ourselves, for divine origins and ends can only be comprehended by one who has access to all things, i.e., by one who is divine.

This mystery bears a remarkable resemblance to the leaves blowing in the wind. As I look around myself, I can see leaves skipping over the pavement, spinning into circles and rising on little thermals. They gather at the base of a tree trunk and then are blown around it, taken down the street. I do not know where the leaves are going, or what purpose they have. I am not even aware of most of them. Analogously, I do not know where the Spirit has come from or where he is going. I am often unaware of him. But one thing I do know: the leaves are present with me. I can scoop them up in my hands and press their papery texture through my fingers. I can crush and crumble them and toss them to the wind again. I can see the wind everywhere moving them as they flap in the canopy or twitch in the long hair of the grass. They are present.

3. Berkhof, *Systematic Theology*, 461.

I have no doubt. Analogously, but in a far more profound spiritual sense, I know the Spirit is with me. I see him moving in the souls around me, stirring hearts and minds with a passion for Christ and a love for the Father. I do not see the Spirit himself, but I do see his effects, as clearly as I see the effects of the wind. Though I do not know where he has come from and where he is going, I try to enjoy the mystery. Mystery, after all, should never dissolve our faith; it should call us forward in worship. Mystery should help us meditate on what we have been given: the very presence of God.

The wind in the trees is thus another quiet testament to God's presence in the ordinary. The eternal, mysterious, triune God is at work to reveal himself in the world around us. As the trees sway in the wind, I look up, and I remember: I do not know where God has come from or where he is going, but I know he is present with me, and that he has purposes ahead of me that I cannot see, just as I cannot see the leaves that have blown down the street. The weather of the world may seem wild and unwieldy, but it is a wondrous testimony to the personal presence of the Trinity. God is moving, far more swiftly and subtly than the autumn wind. But that does not keep the Holy Spirit from playfully revealing himself in the swaying trees.

Look up toward the canopy. The papery song of autumn echoes a divine melody and movement of the Spirit. This is the world that the Lord has made.

# 9

## Birds on a Telephone Wire

EVERY DAY ON MY drive home, I go through twenty or so traffic lights. There have been a few times when a mass of black birds, which I had not noticed, lifted itself from the telephone wires. A cloud formed from the black specks in the sky as they twisted and turned, waving and diving like a giant flag in the wind. These, I have since learned, are starlings.

Starlings gather into large flocks called murmurations. What has puzzled ornithologists is how great masses of distinct creatures, thousands upon thousands, could move with such synchrony. A thousand-member murmuration can bend and turn like a great tablecloth in the clouds. One study concluded that every starling coordinates all of its movements with those of the seven birds that are closest to it.[1] It is as if a great and intricate game of telephone is being played with their bodies.

Ornithologists also say that the starlings' great wafting movements are almost always in response to a predator. The threat makes them fly. Their synchronous beauty has a preserving purpose. I had not thought of that when I saw hundreds of them sitting on telephone wires.

---

1. Andrea Alfano, "How Do Starling Flocks Create Those Mesmerizing Murmurations?" The Cornell Lab of Ornithology, accessed November 4, 2017, https://www.allaboutbirds.org/how-do-starling-flocks-create-those-mesmerizing-murmurations/.

God, of course, spoke the birds into being at the beginning of time. Like every other part of creation, the birds reflect something of his character. Later, as I thought about the flag of starlings waving in the wind, the Spirit helped me to see the character of God in them.

I was first drawn to the stillness and the movement. The starlings were sitting on the telephone wires before my car approached the traffic light. They were *there*, but I did not notice them. Their stillness kept them cloaked in the wide-open world. I did not notice them until I recognized their movement. Analogously, God is ever present in stillness. And he even calls us to take notice of him in that stillness. The psalmist penned God's words in this light, "Be still, and know that I am God" (Ps 46:10). Why would God call us to be still? God would not call us to do anything that did not, in some way, reflect his own behavior, for we are made in his image and likeness (Gen 1:26). And ever since the fall, we have been called to conform to the image of his Son (Rom 8:29). God calls us to be still because *he* is still. This is very difficult for us, especially when we live in a time of flux and entertainment. We are not often still. The ancient practice of Christian meditation is lost on us.[2] But God is ever present in stillness. In our stillness, we will see more of him.

This does nothing to take away from God's dynamism, his active engagement with the world, or his relationality, the way he relates to us and weaves together all of reality into a relational web according to his singular plan. God, to use some terms from Kenneth Pike, is *static, dynamic, and relational* as Father, Son, and Holy Spirit.[3] We see this as the murmuration of starlings lifts itself out of stillness and takes flight in the sky. That is when I noticed them. We seem bent on noticing the dynamic rather than the static. Perhaps we associate the idea of stillness with a lack of life and vigor. But that is presumptuous, given that God himself—the very source of life and vigor—dwells in stillness. The transition from stillness to movement is captivating, much like the starlings' transition

2. I recommend Martin Laird's *Into the Silent Land.*

3. Pike, *Talk, Thought, and Thing,* 47–52.

from their perch to the sky. But it is captivating not because movement itself is so engaging, but because movement and stillness, like so many things in our world, complement one another. We need stillness to appreciate movement, and movement to draw out our longing for stillness.

In God, movement and stillness are harmonized in a way that transcends our ability to understand. In God, we find stillness and stability just as much as we find dynamism and engagement. The word of the Lord stands forever (Isa 40:8), but the word of the Lord is living and active (Heb 4:12). The endurance of God's Word—its divine stillness or fixity—is not antithetical to its dynamism; it is complementary to it. For our God speaks from eternity (Father) the creative and active Word (Son) in life-giving power (Spirit). He is incomparably still and ineffably active. The starlings reflect that stillness and activity on a creaturely level. In that sense, they reveal the character of God.

Another way in which those starlings reveal God's character is through their wafting movements in the air. If you stare at a flock of starlings for a few minutes, you will notice that their turning and waving is based on a general point. Relative fixity somewhere in the murmuration helps us to see the moves and turns; it is almost like a dance. Without a still point in a murmuration, there would be no synchrony, no dance. True, the still points in a murmuration of starlings are fleeting, transitory. But they are there. They must be. Without a still point, there is no dance.

We tend to notice the work of God when we see both the still point and the dance. Or, to put it differently, we notice God's action when we see a point of intersection. Let me offer an example. Last week, I was reading through Genesis 15, the story of Abraham. In Genesis 15:1, God tells Abraham that he will be his *shield*. Just a few days before I read this, I was drawing up notes on Ephesians 6 in an attempt to help my wife deal with spiritual warfare. We had been focused on the *shield* of faith (Eph 6:16). That Sunday, we heard a sermon in which our pastor discussed Genesis 15:1–6 and Abraham's response of faith. This week, I read an article written by a friend and former teacher concerning exegetical preaching. The text that he was using for an example was Genesis 15:1–6. Over the last two weeks, Genesis 15:1–6 has been one of God's still points in my life. He has used that text to weave together my personal relationship with him, his counsel for my wife, our joint instruction in hearing God's word proclaimed, and my intellectual development. For some, this is mere happenstance. But I know better. This is how our God works: he takes a still point and fixes our attention on it. Then he twists and turns the events in our lives around that still point. And we emerge with wonder at the synchrony of his work.

So, the starlings wafting in the air reveal the character of God in their turning on a still point. A place of relative fixity becomes a central marker for synchrony. Likewise, God takes a still point in our lives and shows us his synchronous movements in our personal redemption. He is *always* working, with grace that waves like a flag in the wind.

The ordinary flight habits of starlings apparently have much to say about the extraordinary nature and work of the living God. I do not know when I will see starlings next, but I will be watching for them, as I will be watching for God in his stillness, praying that I will notice him *before* he moves as well as after, and asking him to help me see *him* as the still point around which my life turns and twists.

# 10

## From Dawn to Daylight

---

AT THE TIME OF my writing this, it is early November. We have just turned the clocks back, and so it is not as dark in the morning as it is later in the winter. As I drive to work, I witness something quite ordinary.

The breaking of dawn and its bleeding into daylight feels like a mighty but silent exhalation of God. As I look toward the east, the sky is a gray-blue, the clouds are darker purple, and the tree line is a black silhouette running across the horizon—not neat and flat, but jagged, as the larger oaks and sycamores raise their heads above the smaller birches and maples. On the cusp of the horizon, there is a very subtle glow of orange, and behind that, a whisper of red.

A few minutes later, the edges of the clouds have taken on a pink border that melts into their dark purple center. The subtle glow of orange is now tinted with the same shade of pink. The whisper of red is growing more audible. The light blue slowly overtakes the gray.

Then the pink light at the horizon line becomes bolder, the underbellies of the clouds burn marvelously with a richer pink, and the orange light grows louder. The wisps of cloud that were once tinged with the orange and pink hues are now whiter, proudly so, but amber lingers in their tails that trail back to the breaking skyline.

Minutes later, it is clear: the light is overwhelming the reign of darkness from the night hours. The brilliance of orange spreads through the sky, covering the east and calling out to the west.

At long last, like a piercing eye, the burning circle of the sun peaks over the tree line and throws itself, unhindered, into the waking atmosphere. The clouds are aflame, and only their creases show the darker purple of the earlier dawn. Many of the thinner clouds are nearly all white. The world has awoken.

The whole symphonic process of light spreading over this part of the earth takes a little over an hour. And by its end, the day is the day, and the sunrise is another memory in the mind of God. What strikes me in all of this is the *process*—the daily, repeated process. Every process has a beginning and an end, and we can be tempted to think that the transitory is somehow less important to God. After all, if God is likened to an artist, would he not treasure things that do not so quickly step off the cobblestone present and tread the overgrown grass of the past?

I believe that question is misinformed, for God loves the *craft* of creation and providence. His passion, it seems to me, is not just in the product, the "perfect" moment of a sunrise, but in the process, the symphonic movement from dawn to daylight. The craft itself, the process, is stored in his eternal, divine memory.

There is a British sculptor named Andy Goldsworthy, whose work I have followed over the years.[1] They say that he creates "site-specific land art." He goes out into the world and creates something that lasts only for a short time. His pictures document his work, but the work itself leaves the world just as quickly as it enters. Part of the beauty of his work lies in its ephemerality. There is something striking about working so hard to produce something so beautiful that is yet so fleeting. It moves me deeply.

In a world that is so product-oriented, it is refreshing to find people who love processes, who love the *craft* of something. In my own life, I am guilty of looking forward to products, especially in my writing. I anticipate finishing an essay or article or book,

---

1. Some of his work can be found here: http://visualmelt.com/Andy-Goldsworthy; and here: http://www.artnet.com/artists/andy-goldsworthy/.

imagining the thrill and satisfaction I will feel when I hold it in my hands. But the thrill and satisfaction are short-lived. And to carry on this way is exhausting, for one is never content. The soul sets its sights on a new product before it has even cherished the one right before it. This is the same corruption that materialism breeds. To find true joy in your craft, you must learn to love the process. You must learn to love *not* being finished. This is a lesson that I am still taking in.

Other authors have expressed something similar. I once heard a radio interview with Karl Ove Knausgaard, the Scandinavian author I mentioned in another chapter. He was asked if he found that his writing, which often draws attention to the sanctity of the ordinary, leads him to see the world in a profoundly different way, as if everything looked poetically magnificent to him. The interviewer, in a sense, was asking if the products of his craft, his books, had a great and lasting effect on his perception of the world. His answer was quick and direct: "It's very much the process that's important for me, it's not the result. It's the being in that place where you're questioning the world, or where you see the world, or where you are creating something out of elements from the world . . . that's the place I want to be."[2] Loving the process, the craft—that is what creators should be after.

As I watched the sunrise unfold, I was reminded of how God, in whose image every artist creates, loves the craft. He loves the craft of creation. He loves the craft of providence. He loves the craft of redemption. He loves not just the product, but the process. A little reflection on Scripture shows that this is true.

Consider just one example: Abraham. Here is a man who repeatedly distrusted God and doubted his providential protection, just as we do today. Twice Abraham lied about his marital relationship to save his own skin (Gen 12:10–20; 20). It is no small thing to lie about the most intimate human relationship we possess. He also slept with his wife's servant, Hagar, to find a quicker route to

2. See highlights from the interview here: https://www.npr.org/2017/08/22/545313106/knausgaards-autumn-considers-everything-from-toilet-bowls-to-twilight.

the fulfillment of God's promise (Gen 16:1–4). And yet, in all of this, God does not leave him to his sinful self. Promises are reaffirmed, encouragement is extended, and the promises are one day fulfilled (Gen 21:1–7). All of these peaks and valleys are part of the *craft* of Abraham's redemption, the process through which God is working to redeem him.

Now, why would God do this? Although a specific answer to that question is beyond us, we must at least say that God *wills* Abraham's redemption. It is something God *desires*. God could have made Abraham holy and faithful in an instant. But he did not; he chose the process of redemption. He chose the craft. Just as God willed to make creation a craft, a process through which the world would be spoken into being, so also he wills redemption to be a craft, a process through which the world is re-created. What is true for Abraham is true for each one of us. God loves to craft our lives. He wills the long and sometimes painful process of shaping us to the image of his Son (Rom 8:29).

This does not mean that God does not love the consummation toward which redemptive history is moving. Far from it—God desires to be with his people in unbroken fellowship, as we see plainly throughout all of Scripture. But we often forget the craft. We seek ways to avoid it and jump to the final product. That is not the way God has willed to work.

The sunrise that I witnessed was a beautiful testament to this truth. In that sense, no sunrise is ordinary. Let me say it again: There is no such thing as "ordinary" in God's world. Every morning, in every part of the world, God reaffirms his will to work through process. Each morning, light pushes its way through the darkness, illuminating the clouds, and the trees, and the streets. Each morning, the dawn works its way towards daylight. God wills the subtlety of light curving over the globe. He wills the *time* it takes for the light to crown the treetops and trickle down to the lower branches.

In a more profound way, he wills our continual redemption, our sanctification. He wills the breath of the Spirit working in us to bring new life (John 6:63). He wills the light of his Son to dawn on

49

the darkened valley of each human soul (Matt 4:15–16; John 8:12). He wills the growing brilliance of his own Fatherhood upon us (Rom 8:15; Gal 4:4–6). He wills the great waves of time that draw us closer to the place where he burns in unapproachable light (1 Tim 6:16), and yet calls us to commune with him at the end of all things. We are in the middle of the dawn . . . yes. The great craftsman carries on his work of soul revival and moves patiently in us as the light grows steadily brighter.

# 11

## The Sun on My Cheek

WITH NOVEMBER COMES EARLY nightfall. When I am driving home in the late afternoon, the sun is going down in the west. I drive north, so the sun glare comes straight through the driver's side window. Many of the cars around me bend their visors to block the glare. But I cannot bring myself to do this. I want the light. I want the sun on my cheek.

It is very difficult to describe this feeling. Especially in the colder days of autumn and winter, the sun does not strike or hit the skin; it touches, with rose-petal fingers. The warmth of the light gathers itself and grows bolder, like a flower blooming in silence, keeping its head high as long as you let it. I like to let it.

So often, we block the phenomena around us as if they were *things*, neutral and natural processes to be waved away. But the world is not impersonal processes. The world is not things. Rather, the world is full of fibers and follicles, elements and molecules, organisms and ecosystems—every one of them a reflection of the intimately personal God who spoke them into motion and sustains them with his Word (Gen 1; Heb 1:3). The world whispers of God; it is a speaking world. But this is often lost on us. Why?

That is a difficult question, and I am not wise enough to answer it. But it does at least seem clear that everything in the world is *interpreted*. Nothing simply *is*. Everything *is* according to the interpretation of the one perceiving it. In other words, our world is not only capable of interpretation; it requires interpretation. And here is the rub: there is no such thing as a neutral interpreter.

The wider world scoffs at such a statement. But this does nothing to remove objectivity from the world. It merely calls attention to the way in which we are constituted as observers of our surroundings.[1] This is rooted in the fact that the Trinity is the ultimate observer of creation, and he sees it from every perspective. In John Frame's words, the Trinity is *omniperspectival*.[2] The Trinity is also exhaustively *personal*. God simply is the three persons—Father, Son, and Holy Spirit—in one essence. He is personal in a way that transcends our categories and descriptions of human personhood. This exhaustively personal God created the world in which we live and interpreted it, that is, gave it meaning in relation to *himself*. God interpreted the world, and then called us, as his image bearers, to re-interpret it according to his revelation.[3] But we have a choice, a free will, to choose whether we will interpret the world this way or in some other way.

All of this sounds hopelessly abstract. But think about the implications. When we look to give meaning to the world, we *choose* how we will see it. This does not mean that our understanding of the world constitutes the world as such, in some neo-Kantian

1. I am drawing here on Kenneth Pike's teaching about *observer perspectives*. See also Hibbs, "Do You See How I See?" 59–76.

2. Frame, "A Primer on Perspectivalism (Revised 2008)." Elsewhere he writes, "Theologians say that because God made everything and remembers what he has made, he is omniscient. But his knowledge includes not only basic facts about the trees and the hairs and the sparrows. He sees all these things from every possible *perspective*. He sees the sparrow from behind its head as well as in front of its face. And he sees my hair from its follicle to its ever decreasing pigment. He sees it from his omniscient divine perspective, but he also understands fully how my wife experiences my hair. And he is able to see it as anyone else sees it, from every possible vantage point. He knows what the sparrow looks like to another sparrow, or to the hawk soaring overhead. He sees my hair from the vantage point of the fly on the wall of my office. He even knows perspectives that are merely possible: he knows what my hair *would* look like from the vantage point of a fly on the wall, even when there is no fly on my wall. So God is not only omniscient but omniperspectival." Frame, *Theology in Three Dimensions*, 5.

3. Van Til, *The Defense of the Faith*, 32, 70.

sense. We do not perceive a world of our own making. Rather, we are given the choice to perceive the world as revelatory of the triune, personal God who made it and has a purpose for it or as *brute*, that is, as impersonal and void of personally endowed purpose. People fall at one end or the other, or they fall somewhere in between. But for most of us, even Christians, our default interpretive setting is "brute."

This is because we live in a sinful world that suppresses the clear revelation of God in willful rebellion (Rom 1:18–21). We live in a world that chooses not to see everything around us as God has made it. Instead, we often choose to see all things with imagined "objectivity," which is really nothing more than subjectivism guised by consensus (a consensus held by the majority of those who do not believe in God). Again, this is not to say that there is not objectivity. There most certainly is! But it is *God's* objectivity, not some list of conclusions arrived at by rational principles emptied of personal assumptions. Indeed, we can never empty our perception of personal assumptions, precisely because we cannot empty ourselves of personhood!

Somewhere along the way, we seem to have given ourselves over to this brute, impersonal view of the world. We interpret what we see around us not with reference to the tripersonal God but in feigned isolation from him. That is why we think that the sun on our cheek is just an effect of photons moving through the atmosphere. If that is how we view the sun on our cheek, then we have given ourselves over to an impersonal view of the world. And that view of the world, according to Scripture, is not simply harmful or skewed; it is *false*. If you do not see the tripersonal God reflected in the sunlight, you have not seen the world as it truly is: a reflection of God's character and Lordship.

That is not to say that all of the drivers around me at 4:30pm are godless heathens who are blind to reality. Some of them might be, but that is not the point. The point is that perceiving the world as it was created and is governed by the personal, divine speech of the Trinity brings us to different interpretations, different meanings, for the elements around us. The sun on my cheek is *more* than photons. Our world runs deeper than physicality. It goes deep down to the mysterious and loving Father, Son, and Holy Spirit. *This* God is at the base of reality. *This* God has given everything around us person-oriented purpose according to his divine plan. *This* God is the meaning of the world. That is why Paul writes in Romans 11:36, "from him and through him and to him are all things. To him be glory forever. Amen."

When the soft light of the sun touches my cheek, I enjoy the feeling of warmth, which is a physical effect of God's creation. But I *interpret* that warmth as the natural world's way of saying "Amen" to God's glory. The sunlight on my cheek is the glorious grace of God, another event in my day that tells me of his care and concern for me, his hearth of communion for souls shuddering in isolation. The light is warm on my cheek because God burns with love for his people, for God himself *is* love (1 John 4:8).

I know that most of the other drivers on my evening commute are not seeing the light this way. If they were, I do not think they would pull down their visors and shield their eyes from it. They likely are viewing the light as *mere* light, interpreting God's world impersonally, not being mindful of the richly personal meaning behind every event, every detail, every moment. We are all guilty of it.

This might be one of the most pervasive spiritual problems of our time. Because of it, we are often blind, deaf, and dumb. We do not see the world as it really is. We do not hear the world as it really is. And we do not speak of the world as it really is. We see, hear, and speak in ignorance. We go about our business disengaged from divine personhood, from the ever-present revelation of Father, Son, and Spirit.

But that does not keep God from shining. He lets the sun fall on all of those window visors. He lets people drive on in hiding from him. Not because he is callous, but because he is patient. The Father is waiting for us. And as he waits, he speaks. In back of the evening sunset, sending forth light and warmth, is the Father sending forth his Word (John 1:1) in the power of the Holy Ghost, encouraging us to warm ourselves by his presence. I let the light shine on my face because I like to experience the speech of God in a world that shamelessly believes he is mute.

Oh the things that God can say with a little sunlight.

# 12

## The Sound of Sibilants

My family used to take vacations to Chatham, a little town in Cape Cod, Massachusetts. It was a long drive from the Poconos, where we grew up, about seven hours. My brothers and I would bring our pillows with us. While the sun was still rising, we would settle into our spot in the van. And after an hour or so, when the thrill of a road trip had tapered, we would each fall asleep against a window.

One of my most vivid memories from those trips was not the landscapes and towns we drove through, though I remember many of those too. It was the sibilants. Sibilants are hissing sounds. In English, the most prominent is the letter *s*. We produce this sound by touching the middle of our tongue to the ridge on the roof of our mouth as air is pushed through our teeth. It is a voiceless sound: no vibration from the vocal chords.

For some reason, when you are falling asleep, your ears will continue to catch the sibilants in the speech around you. I can still remember the exchange of sibilants between my mother and father as we meandered up the east coast on Route 487, through the broad, green hills of Connecticut. I did not know what they were talking about. Most of the consonant and vowel sounds fell into the background, overtaken by the hum of the van's engine. But those sibilants—I could listen to those for hours.

Looking back, I believe the sibilants were deeply comforting to me because they revealed the presence of my parents. When you are a child, parents can seem like giants, superhumans that can manage and navigate the wild world. You trust them, even in situations that would appear to be well beyond their control. Sleeping in the car with the sound of my parents' sibilants drifting into the backseats—that was when I was truly a child.

Of course, the sundry speech sounds we have in English, and in every other language, ancient and modern, were all manifested first in the mind of God. As my friend and teacher wrote, "God's wisdom in language is unfathomable."[1] It is unfathomable now, with all of the dialects and discourse floating through the air across the great globe at any given moment, but it is also unfathomable in eternity past. It was then (if we can even use the word "then") that God had all of the sibilants stored up for use by creatures whom he knew would rebel against him. He had all of the letters, all of the sounds, stored in his mind—a great and variegated alphabet.

I once read an essay by F. W. Boreham in which he reflected on toy birthday blocks with letters on them. With Revelation 1:8 and 22:13 in mind, no doubt, he writes,

> "I am—*Alpha and Omega!*" "I am—*A and Z!*" "I am—*the Alphabet!*" . . . I take these birthday blocks that came to our house today and strew the letters on my study floor. So far as any spiritual significance is concerned, they seem as dead as the dry bones in Ezekiel's Valley. And yet "*I am the Alphabet!*" "Come," I cry, with the prophet of the captivity, "come from the *Four Winds*, O Breath, and breathe upon these slain that they may live!" And the prayer has scarcely escaped my lips when lo, all the letters of the alphabet shine with a wondrous luster and glow with a profound significance.[2]

That luster and glow emerges from the divine mind itself. The letter *s* is not just a consonant. It is something that was stored in God's mind, brought out in pronunciation through a host of languages, in a host of times, in a host of places.

---

1. Poythress, *God-Centered Biblical Interpretation*, 151.
2. Boreham, *A Packet of Surprises*, 6.

And here is what pulls me most: that quietude in the van on my childhood trips to Chatham is a reflection of the eternal quietude in which God dwells, muttering the trialogue of Father, Son, and Spirit while an infant creation drifts off to sleep in the back seat of the cosmos, well on its way to unending communion with the God who speaks.

Oh, it can be so easy to believe that God has been torn away from the world—that sibilants are just sibilants. Sounds are mere sounds. Light is light and death is death. But there is a God who is ever present with us, and if we quiet ourselves before his word, before his speech, we will hear holy sibilants: sounds that catch the ear of the soul and remind us that we are and always will be *children*, and that our great God is speaking to himself as he bends the world to his intended ends. May we all fall asleep in that.

# 13

## Is This My Thumb?

RAISING A TWO-YEAR-OLD PRESENTS many opportunities to re-discover all of the raw experiences we have forgotten as adults. Balancing your body on your feet, using utensils and fine motor skills, washing out a cut with soap and water, learning a word for something in the world—these are the life lessons of a two-year-old. But they are my life lessons, too.

Nora was trying to color a picture from her coloring book, scraping a mechanical pencil over the dull surface with noticeable frustration. "Doesn't work . . ." she whined, as she hobbled over to my office chair, straddling her feet a few inches wider than her tiny shoulders.

"Oh, here," I said, taking the pencil from her dimpled fist. "See this top part?" "Ya," she muttered. "You push this down and then . . . the lead comes out the bottom. Can you see it?" "Ya," she said again, reaching for the pencil.

I watched as she tried to push the top of the pencil with her index finger. "Mmmmm"— Nora's classic grumbling noise. "Here, let me see. . . . You have to use your thumb." Nora looked straight up at me with her giant brown eyes and offered her hand, along with a beautiful little question: "'Dis my thumb?"

I was not expecting that. I guess I thought she already knew what her thumb was from reading books and hearing conversations. I had never told her that this little opposable protrusion on her hand was called a "thumb."

She ran off after that, dropping the pencil to play with something else. But I sat in the chair staring at my own hands, wiggling my thumbs and watching the wrinkles gather and stretch as I bent my knuckles. "This is my thumb," I said to myself. "This is my thumb."

Nora's question, like many questions of young children, made me reassess something very basic to our experience: that we have parts of our body, that they are distinguishable from each other, that we have created sounds and matched them to each body part so that we can talk about them. That final point traces back not just to human anatomy, but to what we might call divine anatomy: the character and nature of God himself.

God is a speaking being, I have frequently emphasized, but he is also a *naming* being.[1] He names himself, he names the world, and he names us. But more than this, he created us in his image as speaking creatures and told us to name reality (Gen 2:19–20). All of our naming is a reflection of the one who names.

First, God names himself. He does so in many ways, but I enjoy focusing on the more explicitly *personal* way in which he names himself. We might call it *generational naming*, when God names himself as the God of previous generations. Frequently in the books of Genesis and Exodus, God names himself according to the personal relationships he has held with his creatures in prior generations. He is the God of Abraham, Isaac, and Jacob (Gen 32:9; Exod 3:6, 15–16; 4:5). He is the God of Israel, the God of Moses, the God of David.

To make this even more personal, we might say, "He is the God of _____." Fill in that blank with the name of any believer in the history of the world. He is the God of Donald Ray

---

1. Hibbs, "Words for Communion," 5–8; "Closing the Gaps," 299–322; *The Speaking Trinity & His Worded World: Why Language Is at the Center of Everything* (forthcoming from Wipf & Stock).

Hibbs (my late father). He is the God of Donald Shepherd Hibbs (my late grandfather). He is the God of his *persons*, his saved and sanctified souls, born by his very breath, renewed by that breath in the name of Christ. *He is the God of his own.*

And the naming ability he has given to us reflects him. A name, after all, *contrasts* who we are with who we are not, just as our heavenly Father is contrasted from creation as Lord of all. A name also is always *instantiated*: taking on syntax in a sentence, or phonemes in a conversation. There is no bare name in abstraction, just as there is no bare God in abstraction. God is eternally instantiated in the Word, the perfect and profound expression of the Father's thought. And that Word was instantiated in our world, taking on flesh, bones, and blood. Lastly, a name is always *distributed* in real and raw contexts. The context provides a home for a name, where it can be heard with consistent clarity, just as the Holy Spirit is the personal context for the names "Father" and "Son" in their eternal love. All names are deeply trinitarian.[2]

Second, God names the world around us. The day, the night, the heavens, the seas—God titled them in his own tongue.[3] The fundamental borders of existence (light and darkness, air and water) were *called* by God. He gave sounds to substance and in so doing brought out their uniqueness (contrast), gave us a means to identify them when we encountered them (instantiation) in their context within the uttered world (distribution).

Third, God names us. Though he named Adam directly, he named the rest of us indirectly by governing the linguistic capabilities of every one of Adam's progeny. It is true that sometimes he

2. The triad of contrast/variation/distribution comes from the language theory of Kenneth L. Pike. The related triad of classification/instantiation/association comes from Vern Poythress. See Pike, *Language in Relation to a Unified Theory of the Structure of Human Behavior*; *Linguistic Concepts*; Poythress, "Reforming Ontology and Logic in the Light of the Trinity," 187–219; *God-Centered Biblical Interpretation.*

3. Though we have access to the Hebrew names from Genesis 1, we do not know if God actually used the Hebrew language or if he used his own divine language, which the biblical writer then recorded in Hebrew. Either one is possible. Even if God did use something like the Hebrew language, it would still have been *his own* language at that point, since humans had not been created yet.

decided to intervene and rename certain of his people (Abram, Sarai, Jacob) to express his plans for them or his history with them, a sort of divine editing. And in the New Testament, he was directly responsible for naming both John and Jesus (Luke 1:13, 31). But on the whole, God was pleased to have his people name their children, letting them take up the holy responsibility of using language to contrast creatures in the world, to aid us in identifying them as they were instantiated in it, and to relate them to a contextual web of divine providence.

That brings in the final point: God passed on the divine act of naming to his image bearers. We name not only our children but also places, objects, concepts, emotions, body parts, and so on. In giving this ability to us, God entrusted us with the task of verbally setting apart elements in the world (contrast). "Thumb" stands apart from "ring finger" and "pinky." He entrusted us with enabling others to identify thumbs whenever they came across them (instantiation). My thumb is different from my wife's, my daughter's, my son's. But they are all thumbs. He also entrusted us with the ability to relate these named elements to one another in a verbal network of functional relationships (distribution). "Thumb" goes with "fingers" and "hands" and "knuckles," so that I can utter the sentence, "Of all the fingers on my hand, my thumb has the biggest knuckle." That little sentence has meaning because of the name-giving God, who controls not only the names we give to elements in the world but how those very elements are related to each other and to his greater plan of redemption.

Naming, as it turns out, is no small gift from God. By it, we reflect the character of our naming Creator, the one who *called* all things in relation to himself as Father, Son, and Spirit. In naming, we demarcate (Father), identify (Son), and relate (Spirit).

In light of this, I am sure that God is deeply concerned with our naming of fingers, not because we are especially talented or witty, but because God sees himself in us. God heard Nora utter her innocent question that morning, and he did not just see a two-year-old expanding her vocabulary; he saw *himself*. He saw little

Nora imaging *him*. It is a wonder such daily phenomena go unnoticed by us, when they hold God's attention for eternity.

"Thumb," I say to myself once more. "Yes, this is my thumb."

## 14

# Falling Snow

In early December of this year, I watch the first snow. Millions of tiny ice stars float through the air, strike the pavement and sidewalk, and soften into water. White is lost to black in the pavement, or gray in the cement, or yellow in the dying grass. So many stars disappearing so quickly, and without a sound . . .

Snow is the humblest weather. It makes no name for itself, but enters in silence, in the background of the world's stage, and gathers itself only to accent what is already here: rounding the roofs of houses and cars, blunting the corners of the curbs, mirroring upside-down arcs of maple limbs, which stay utterly still, like extended fingers. The snow takes the shape of the world, meekly laying itself down to draw attention to the truth and fixity of a landscape.

As I stare at the snow falling, I feel subtly overwhelmed. "There is too much," I think, "too much to take in, too much to account for." I follow a few of the flakes with my eyes, watching them drift from the height of the porch ceiling down to the frozen flowerbed. Then I fix my eyes on the neighbor's yard, watching the white flecks cover his green and brown grass. For a few moments, I forget about time. Greatness is meant to leave us dazed, I think.

Elihu, one of Job's friends, once said,

> God thunders wondrously with his voice;
> he does great things that we cannot comprehend.

For to the snow he says, 'Fall on the earth,'

likewise to the downpour, his mighty downpour.

(Job 37:5–6)

It is divine speech that is responsible for the snow falling outside. God says, "Fall," and water molecules respond. The inanimate world is still, in a mysterious sense, in dialogue with God. It has no will of its own, and yet it does the bidding of the one who addresses it. The world is a bound recipient of God's speech.

And God, as speaker, has ordained where every one of these ice stars outside my window is going to land: on the sidewalk, along the telephone wires, on the limbs of our neighbor's sycamore tree. I cannot keep track of the snow, but he already has—the ephemerality of every flake. God's holy language controls all.

That is what makes the humility of snow so remarkable. The God of unrivalled power is its verbal source. Behind an earthly silence, there is a heavenly speech so potent that it goes beyond all our attempts at understanding it. In fact, its potency goes beyond our attention. We are so overwhelmed, so completely governed by it, that we do not notice it. In God's wisdom, the silent and unnoticed is far louder and conspicuous than we imagine. But we do not have the ears to hear it or the eyes to see it.

This is one of the many wonders I have of God. He seems bent on funneling his raw power and unbridled greatness through almost pitiable weakness. These infinitesimal specks, these snowflakes—that the greatness of God should be behind soft and brittle bits of water! But this is simply who he is: the three-personed mysterious Lord who saw fit to redeem the world not by dominating in his majesty but by dying in our flesh. Who would have predicted that redemption for a hideous human race would come by giving rather than taking?

And so, behind the falling snow is the voice of the Trinity. The world does his bidding. While that in itself may not seem so mysterious, I am baffled at the contrast between his might and his means, between his power and the marks of his presence. So soft a precipitation as snow could not possibly reflect the presence of a

God who is sharply holy, and yet it does. Many times, he chooses the soft and the subtle to humble the coarse and the crude—not so unlike the way in which this snow is blanketing the landscape, making the heavy world seem lighter, almost weightless, as if the entirety of history could come to a close this afternoon with a single word.

# 15

## Light around the Window Shades

GREAT POWER LIES IN subtlety. In God's world, it is not just the grand that gathers us, but the slight and the small.

I awoke before my wife this morning and turned my head toward the windows, staring at the light creeping in around the shades. On the left side of two windows facing east, and on both sides of the window facing west, the light was gray-white, sharp and clean. On the right side of the two east-facing windows, where the warmth from the sunrise came more directly, a pale gold light hovered, almost patiently.

As I laid there, I thought of how a whole world of light was just waiting to get into our room. It had been there before my eyes opened. And now, without calling much attention to itself, the light would wait until we drew up the shades.

Light, of course, is inanimate. It does not "wait" and cannot be "patient." But God is behind the light, ever using the turning world to reveal himself. The light is not patient, but I could see God's patience *in* it—his great quietness, his omnipotent meekness hovering outside the window. In a sense, those slits of light around the window shades felt like words, ancient words, so old and simple that I could hardly hear them. I stared and listened closely for a few minutes. And I believe the words were "I am."

It is not difficult to see why I hardly heard them. To say that something *is* does not tell us very much, does it? We want more than *is*. *Is*, we assume, adds nothing to silence. It is barely revelatory.

But why, then, would God reveal himself as *I am*? When Moses begged God to tell him his name so that he could approach the elders of Israel with a backbone, God gave him *I am* as his name (Exod 3:14). "I am who I am" is the way many translations have it. That sounds somewhat hollow to us today. "Lord," "Savior," "Redeemer," "Creator"—these names have immediate connotations. As soon as they ring in our ears, associations leap into the foreground of our mind. But not so with "I am." Why?

This is even more puzzling and profound when we consider the seven metaphorical "I am" statements from Jesus Christ in the Gospel of John: "I am the bread of life" (6:35); "I am the light of the world" (8:12); "I am the door of the sheep" (10:7); "I am the good shepherd" (10:11); "I am the resurrection and the life" (11:25); "I am the way, the truth, and the life" (14:6); "I am the true vine" (15:1). These statements, we think, are much different. The subject is linked to an easily recognized complement in each case. But these claims of Jesus are easier for us to process only because we do not typically break them down. We read them as chunks.

But what if we were to break them down? Take the claim of John 6:35, for instance. We can take each word and look more closely.

> *I.* That's just a pronoun. There's nothing marvelous or mysterious about pronouns. Or is there? Pronouns are rooted in God himself, for God is three persons who can each say *I, thou*, and *he*.[1] There are pronouns because of the Father, Son, and Holy Spirit. The triune God created us in his image, so every time we hear or read a pronoun, we hear or read something that has been created and sustained out of God's own character. Pronouns are deeply personal and wondrously mysterious.

> *Am.* The verb *to be* is one of the most common words in the English language. That means it is most susceptible to being thought about the least in everyday usage. What

1. Hodge, *Systematic Theology*, 1:444.

does it mean "to be"? We are back at the Exodus 3:14 issue. "To be" sounds hopelessly abstract. If we say it means "to exist," we have scarcely improved our situation. But I would say that this verb is rooted in God's character. Long before all the things that we recognize around us, things that we say "are" or "exist," God was there: three persons in holy and unbroken communion. So, "to be" in an ultimate sense is not just some impersonal state. That is not the divinely instated semantic origin of the word. No, to be is to be in *communion*, to be in relationship.[2] God *is* Father, Son, and Spirit. Existence has not been derived from an impersonal explosion, but from tripersonal speech. So, "to be" is profoundly personal and relational.

*the bread of life.* Let's look at this last phrase as a unit. "Bread" is a concrete noun we can wrap our minds around. It has a deep history in our world. Yet, adding the prepositional phrase "of life" complicates things a bit. Not only is there a varied substance that is manifested by mixing elements and heat, but there is a sort of substance that gives "life." What is "life," really? Again, we must resist saying something like "existence." That does not get us anywhere. "Life" is rooted in the character of God. God is the God of the living (Mark 12:27), but before he created anything, he was still the *living* God. He was still a loving and glorious communion of divine persons. "Life" connotes not some bare existence, but a *relational* existence, one that is tied to persons. For Jesus to claim that he is the bread of life means, among other things, that he is the only one who can deliver us into an eternal personal communion, a restored and everlasting *relationship* with God and with his people.

In saying "I am the bread of life," Jesus would still be communicating something wondrously personal if he stopped with "I am." For the Son of God to come in the flesh and simply *be* is nothing short of miraculous. It is the divine, eternal God entering into time and space: the origin of personhood standing on the Mediterranean

2. Greshake, "Trinity as 'Communio,'" 331–45.

dirt of a person-centered world—a world that everywhere reflects the character of the God who spoke it.

When we return to the Exodus 3:14 title for God, "I am," we see that this is not some philosophical abstraction meant solely to show us our intellectual limitations. It does that, certainly, but it does so much more. It points us to a relational God, a God who is relational in himself and who also spoke a world into motion that exists as a reflection of his character in a million ways, and thus a world that is always and everywhere related to *him*.

You see, *to be* is profoundly personal. To be is to live and move *in God* (Acts 17:28). The light around my window shades can easily go unnoticed, but so can just *being there*. It is no small thing to be. To be is profoundly personal because to be is always to hold a relationship with the God who is relational in himself. To be is to have presence and to find stability in the sustaining speech of God (Heb 1:3), who eternally "speaks" with himself.

I say again, great power lies in subtlety, and it does so because power is rooted in the personal, relational presence of God himself, who sustains every fiber of the world with his word. The light around the window shades is a silent reminder that God is always preceding us with his own personal presence.

# Epilogue

Sometimes I wonder if people who read my work think that I am advocating for some sort of pantheism, as if God were identified with the world he created and everything in it were divine. That, hopefully, is clearly *not* what I have been doing in this book. I have simply made an attempt to find God in the ordinary, to look at the world around me and experience his presence. In my opinion, if we do not do this, there are several implications for our faith.

First, there is the obvious danger of our becoming ignorant of or even immune to God's presence. Scripture tells us very clearly that God is ever-present (Ps 139). There is nowhere that we can go to flee from him. But the follow up question must be, *how is God present in the world?* We cannot simply claim that God is ever-present and then not articulate *how*. I have argued, in a long line of Reformed thinkers including John Calvin, that God is present via his revelation. The whole world, all that has been made (Rom 1:18–21), reveals God. This is nothing novel. But it seems novel, perhaps because we live during the philosophical aftermath of movements such as the Enlightenment, rationalism, and empiricism.[1]

Second, if we do not search for God in the ordinary, we do not perceive the world as it truly is. God has revealed that his

---

1. These are movements that view the world as impersonal. They ignore or significantly downplay God's presence. See Frame, *A History of Western Philosophy and Theology*, 177–207; 214–16.

entire creation manifests his character. Psalm 19:1–4, as we saw, is a clear testament to this:

> The heavens declare the glory of God,
> and the sky above proclaims his handiwork.
> Day to day pours out speech,
> and night to night reveals knowledge.
> There is no speech, nor are there words,
> whose voice is not heard.
> Their voice goes out through all the earth,
> and their words to the end of the world.

The whole earth, every crevice of creation, has been endowed by God himself with a revelatory component. We can choose to ignore this component if we wish, but then we will not be seeing the world as it truly is. We will be seeing a world of our own making. And when we make our own worlds, they fall painfully short of the glory that God deserves.

Third, if we do not search for God in the ordinary, we will miss very precious parts of life. The mediums of sitcom and drama, as well as film, have quietly convinced us that life is made up of momentous events that we rush to, and all in between them is dead space. We rush from thrill to thrill, possession to possession, weekend to weekend, treating the intermittent time as something to be tread, like water in a swimming pool. The fact that we are immersed in the ordinary does not mean that it is vapid of revelation. We will not see this revelation without the lens of Scripture, but that does not change the fact that the world is revelatory, that the world speaks of God in the sense that it reveals his character and purposes. If we rush ahead to what we deem "extraordinary," we will miss a wealth of "ordinary" gifts, precious gifts, that God is giving to us every day. These are, if you like, gifts of his own self-communication. They are opportunities for us to "hear" him addressing us as image-bearers; they are opportunities for us to respond in prayerful adoration.

If nothing else, I hope this little book has helped you to think of the *extraordinary* ordinary in your own life. Mark my words, God is here. And he is not hidden, as some liberal theologians would like us to believe. We only think he is hidden because we are all recovering from blindness. This world is a treasure chest beneath our feet; we tread over it thoughtlessly. My prayer for you is the same as the prayer I have uttered to God many times: "My God, open my eyes to see what is all around me so that I might be more conscious of the truth that I live and move and breath *in* you."

# Bibliography

Bavinck, Herman. *Reformed Dogmatics*. Vol. 2, *God and Creation*. Edited by John Bolt. Translated by John Vriend. Grand Rapids, MI: Baker Academic, 2004.

Berkhof, Louis. *Systematic Theology*. New ed. Grand Rapids, MI: William B. Eerdmans, 1996.

Calvin, John. *Institutes of the Christian Religion: A New Translation of the 1541 Edition*. Translated by Robert White. Carlisle, PA: Banner of Truth, 2014.

Frame, John M. *The Doctrine of God*. A Theology of Lordship. Phillipsburg, NJ: P&R, 2002.

———. *The Doctrine of the Knowledge of God*. A Theology of Lordship. Phillipsburg, NJ: P&R, 1987.

———. *The Doctrine of the Word of God*. A Theology of Lordship. Phillipsburg, NJ: P&R, 2010.

———. *A History of Western Philosophy and Theology*. Phillipsburg, NJ: P&R, 2015.

———. *Systematic Theology: An Introduction to Christian Belief*. Phillipsburg, NJ: P&R, 2013.

Greshake, Gisbert. "Trinity as 'Communio.'" In *Rethinking Trinitarian Theology: Disputed Questions and Contemporary Issues in Trinitarian Theology*, edited by Robert J. Woźniak and Giulio Maspero, 331–45. London: T&T Clark, 2012.

Hibbs, Pierce Taylor. "Closing the Gaps: Perichoresis and the Nature of Language." *Westminster Theological Journal* 78, no. 2 (Fall 2016) 299–322.

———. "Imaging Communion: An Argument for God's Existence Based on Speech." *Westminster Theological Journal* 77, no. 1 (Spring 2015) 35–51.

———. "Words for Communion." *Modern Reformation* 25, no. 4 (August 2016) 5–8.

Hodge, Charles. *Systematic Theology*. Vol. 1. Peabody, MA: Hendrickson, 2013.

Knausgaard, Karl Ove. *Autumn*. Translated by Ingvild Burkey. New York: Penguin, 2017.

Kuyper, Abraham. *The Work of the Holy Spirit*. Translated by Henry De Vries. Chattanooga, TN: AMG, 1995.

Milgrom, Jacob. "The Alleged 'Hidden Light.'" In *The Idea of Biblical Interpretation: Essays in Honor of James L. Kugel*, edited by Hindy Najman and Judith H. Newman. Boston: Brill, 2004.

Oliphint, K. Scott. *The Majesty of Mystery: Celebrating the Glory of an Incomprehensible God*. Bellingham, WA: Lexham, 2016.

Pike, Kenneth L. *Language in Relation to a Unified Theory of the Structure of Human Behavior*. 2nd ed. The Hague: Mouton, 1967.

———. *Linguistic Concepts: An Introduction to Tagmemics*. Lincoln, NE: University of Nebraska Press, 1982.

———. *Talk, Thought, and Thing: The Emic Road toward Conscious Knowledge*. Dallas, TX: Summer Institute of Linguistics, 1993.

Poythress, Vern S. "God and Language." In *Did God Really Say? Affirming the Truthfulness and Trustworthiness of Scripture*, edited by David B. Garner, 93–106. Phillipsburg, NJ: P&R, 2012.

———. *God-Centered Biblical Interpretation*. Phillipsburg, NJ: P&R, 1999.

———. "God's Lordship in Interpretation." *Westminster Theological Journal* 50 (1988) 27–64.

———. *In the Beginning Was the Word: Language—A God-Centered Approach*. Wheaton, IL: Crossway, 2009.

———. *Redeeming Science: A God-Centered Approach*. Wheaton, IL: Crossway, 2006.

———. "Reforming Ontology and Logic in the Light of the Trinity: An Application of Van Til's Idea of Analogy." *Westminster Theological Journal* 57, no. 1 (Spring 1995) 187–219.

Rilke, Rainer Maria. *Rilke's Book of Hours: Love Poems to God*. Translated by Anita Barrows and Joanna Macy. 100th Anniversary ed. New York: Riverhead, 2005.

Saussure, Ferdinand de. *Course in General Linguistics*. Edited by Charles Bally and Albert Sechehaye. Translated by Wade Baskin. New York: Philosophical Library, 1959.

Sayers, Dorothy L. *The Mind of the Maker*. New York: HarperOne, 1987.

Smith, Mark S. "Light in Genesis 1:3—Created or Uncreated: A Question of Priestly Mysticism." In *Birkat Shalom: Studies in the Bible, Ancient Near Eastern Literature, and Postbiblical Judaism Presented to Shalom M. Paul on the Occasion of His Seventieth Birthday*, edited by Chaim Cohen. Winona Lake, IN: Eisenbrauns, 2008.

Stăniloae, Dumitru. *The Holy Trinity: In the Beginning There Was Love*. Translated by Roland Clark. Brookline, MA: Holy Cross Orthodox Press, 2012.

Van Til, Cornelius. *In Defense of the Faith*. Vol. 2, *A Survey of Christian Epistemology*. Phillipsburg, NJ: Presbyterian and Reformed, 1969.

———. *The Defense of the Faith*. Edited by K. Scott Oliphint. 4th ed. Phillipsburg, NJ: P&R, 2008.

Vos, Geerhardus. *Reformed Dogmatics*. Vol. 2, *Anthropology*. Edited and translated by Richard B. Gaffin Jr. Bellingham, WA: Lexham, 2014.

Waltke, Bruce K. Genesis: A Commentary (Grand Rapids, Mich.: Zondervan, 2001), 61

Lightning Source UK Ltd.
Milton Keynes UK
UKHW021823300419
341886UK00005B/197/P